QUAKER SPIRITUALITY

QUAKER SPIRITUALITY

Selected Writings

Foreword by Rick Moody

Edited by Emilie Griffin and Douglas V. Steere

HarperSanFrancisco

A Division of HarperCollins*Publishers*

The Publisher gratefully acknowledges the use of material from the following books:

The Journal of George Fox, edited by John L. Nichalls. Used by permission of The Library Committee of the Religious Society of Friends in Great Britain.

The Journal and Major Essays of John Woolman, edited by Phillips P. Moulton. Copyright © 1971 by Oxford University Press, Inc. Reprinted by permission.

Finding the Trail of Life by Rufus M. Jones. Copyright 1926 by Macmillan Publishing Co., Inc., renewed 1954 by Mary Hoxie Jones. Reprinted with permission of Macmillan Publishing Co., Inc.

The Luminous Trail by Rufus M. Jones. Copyright 1947 by Macmillan Publishing Co., Inc., renewed 1975 by Mary Hoxie Jones. Reprinted with permission of Macmillan Publishing Co., Inc.

A Testament of Devotion by Thomas R. Kelly. Copyright © 1941 Harper & Row, Publisher, Inc., renewed © 1969 by Lois Lael Kelly Stabler. Reprinted by permission of Harper & Row Publishers, Inc.

The Eternal Promise by Thomas Kelly, edited by Richard M. Kelly. Copyright © 1966 by Richard M. Kelly. Reprinted by permission of Harper & Row, Publishers, Inc.

HarperCollins books may be purchased for educational, business, or sales promotional use. For information please write: Special Markets Department, HarperCollins Publishers, Inc., 10 East 53rd Street, New York, NY 10022.

HarperCollins Web site: http://www.harpercollins.com

HarperCollins®, ✲®, and HarperSanFrancisco™ are trademarks of HarperCollins Publishers, Inc.

Book Design by Susan Rimerman

FIRST EDITION

Library of Congress Cataloging-in-Publication Data is available.
Quaker spirituality : selected writings / foreword by Rick Moody ; edited by Emilie Griffin and Douglas V. Steere. — 1st ed.
p. cm.
ISBN 0–06–057872–6
1. Spirituality—Society of Friends. 2. Society of Friends—Doctrines. I. Griffin, Emilie.
II. Steere, Douglas Van, 1901–1995
BX7738.Q34   2005
248.4'896—dc22   2004060655

05 06 07 08 09 RRD(H) 10 9 8 7 6 5 4 3 2 1

CONTENTS

FOREWORD

I was raised Episcopalian, which is about as far from the Quaker faith as you can get and still be a Protestant. Things I associated with compulsory church attendance when I was a kid in the suburbs—ritual, liturgy, priestly vestments, incense, bells—were manifestly the trappings of Episcopalianism, and when, as a teenager, I rebelled against the church, it was these things that I resisted. In this way I was led to my first encounter with a Quaker meeting. It happened that I also knew a number of people who had been helped inordinately by the recovery movement, and of these there were any number who found their way to Quaker meeting. Why? Because there was no mediating agency between worshiper and God in Quaker meeting. There was no one in the Society of Friends to tell you what you had to do, nor was there a right or wrong way to practice faith there. As with the recovery movement, the Quaker faith seemed to me antiestablishment, even revolutionary. Also antiwar, anti–death penalty, against frippery of any kind. Quakers who dressed for worship seemed either very old-fashioned or out of step.

No wonder that my first experience of Quaker spirituality was of a most welcome liberation. The silence of Quaker meeting, for one, was the silence that I associated with God, but here made entirely positive, even ecstatic. The idea that you would not speak unless the voice of God spoke through you—this seemed refreshing, unprepossessing, and, at least in the context of my spiritual education, innovative. My encounter with Quaker meeting was so overpowering that I quickly took my wife (back then she was just my girlfriend). She found there a spiritual experience completely analogous to the Congregational worship of her childhood in the Midwest. In fact, my wife still attends the Quaker meetings in Brooklyn, where we live, in a lovable and charming meeting-house right downtown, crammed between skyscrapers and the soon-to-be-demolished Brooklyn jail.

If I eventually found my way back to Episcopalianism, it was not for lack of appreciation for the Society of Friends. It's just that my esteem for the Quaker faith became more literary. For after I went to Quaker meeting four or five times, I became interested in the journals of George Fox, the founder of Quakerism. Many readers may be familiar with the broad outline of the Fox narra-tive, how he suffered years of beatings, jailings, and institutional persecution in England for the crime of having conceived of a new method for worship. However, this mean treatment only seemed to embolden Fox, and as the reader will see in the pas-sages that follow here, it only brought out in him further pages of homespun and unpretentious wisdom on how to forge a direct relationship with God: "For this we can say to the whole world, we have wronged no man's person or possessions, we have used no force nor violence against any man." I found George Fox's journals to be some of the best writing in English from the seven-teenth century. After further reflection, I was surprised even more by how consistent the literary accomplishments of the Quaker faith have been since.

Of special interest, for example, are the journals of John Wool-man, one of the early voices of Quakerism on American soil. His journals were very highly regarded by American writers of the transcendental period (Whittier was especially fervent on the subject of Woolman), and with just cause. The Quaker faith, when set loose on a continent known for its infatuation with rugged individualism and resistance to tyranny, seemed to blossom. And Woolman's tales of carrying the message of direct spiritual experience to the colonies ring true, especially in the matter of slavery. Woolman was opposed to the sin of slavery almost a hundred years before the fervent period of abolitionism. His writings on the subject and his willingness to withstand estrangement from his fellow Friends are especially moving: "I, however, believed that liberty was the natural right of all men equally."

Woolman was no less opinionated on the rights of the native population of the North American continent or on the subject of capitalism and profit. He was utterly skeptical about the running of a business in the expectation of profit: "I saw that a humble man with the blessing of the Lord might live on a little, and that where the heart was set on greatness, success in business did not satisfy the craving."

The more contemporary Quaker voices contained herein connect the mystical vision of Fox's unmediated experience of God with the political insight of Woolman. Thomas Kelly's experiences as an elder in the church, for example, make the connection explicit: "The straightest road to social gospel runs through profound mystical experience. The paradox of true mysticism is that individual experience leads to social passion. . . . If we seek a social gospel, we must find it most deeply rooted in the mystic way." In this way,

Quaker spirituality appears remarkably coherent over the three hundred and fifty years of its existence. George Fox had a vision of Christian mission, a vision of Jesus of Nazareth that didn't require the opinions of experts, and in the pursuit of this mission he was led out into the world. In the twenty-first century, our needs are just as keen for this ministry of social and political justice, and how lucky we are that the Quakers, like the Gnostics before them, saw fit to write it all down. The message of the gospel is here in these pages, and you need no further advice from me but that you should go ahead, now, and read.

—RICK MOODY

THE JOURNAL OF
GEORGE FOX

George Fox (1624–1691)

George Fox, whose life and witness were largely responsible for drawing together and setting the pattern of the spirituality of the Religious Society of Friends, was anything but a constant journal keeper. What is here called a journal is really an autobiography and is generally regarded as one of the great religious autobiographies in the English language.

Fox had a prodigious memory, and in one of his long imprisonments in 1664, he either wrote or dictated a detailed account of the seventeen years of his adult life from 1647 to 1664. This is referred to as the Short Journal and was used to refresh his mind when, a decade later, in 1674–1675, he dictated a fuller account to Thomas Lower, his stepson-in-law and devoted companion, who was the husband of one of Margaret Fell's daughters. This fuller account is called the Spence Manuscript. Thomas Ellwood, a gifted Quaker writer, was officially commissioned to take these manuscripts, together with copious letters, pastoral epistles, and other papers, and produce the first full account of Fox's life. This he accomplished in 1694, three years after Fox's death. The Ellwood edition of Fox's Journal was prefaced by a moving tribute to Fox written by William Penn.

The sections of The Journal of George Fox that follow are an abridgment or selection from the 760-page Nickalls edition published by Cambridge University Press in 1952. This edition is regarded as the most accurate and readable one in existence today. The selections open with a few choice passages from William Penn's preface.

—DOUGLAS V. STEERE

Editorial notes:
- Fox applied the term priest to all professional preachers, ministers, and clergy, irrespective of the particular sect to which they belonged.
- Fox often refers to his experiences, especially religious ones, as "openings."
- Leather breeches are mentioned in a number of places. These are the suit of leather that Fox often wore because of its durability and suitability for his rough, outdoor life of travel on horseback.

William Penn's Preface

[Extracts from William Penn's Preface to the Original Edition of George Fox's Journal, 1694]

He was a man that God endued with a clear and wonderful depth, a discerner of others' spirits, and very much a master of his own. And though the side of his understanding which lay next to the world, and especially the expression of it, might sound uncouth and unfashionable to nice ears, his matter was nevertheless very profound; and would not only bear to be often considered but the more it was so the more weighty and instructing it appeared. And abruptly and brokenly as sometimes his sentences would fall from him about divine things, it is well known they were often as texts to many fairer declarations. And indeed it showed, beyond all contradiction, that God sent him, that no arts or parts had any share in his matter or manner of his ministry; and that so many great, excellent, and necessary truths as he came forth to preach to mankind had therefore nothing of man's wit or wisdom to recommend them; so that as to man he was an original, being no man's copy. And his ministry and writings show they are from one that was not taught of man, nor had learned what he said by study. Nor were they notional or speculative, but sensible and practical truths, tending to conversion and regeneration and the setting up of the kingdom of God in the hearts of men; and the way of it was his work.

In his testimony or ministry, he much laboured to open Truth to the people's understandings, and to bottom them upon the principal, Christ Jesus, the Light of the world, that by bringing them to something that was of God in themselves, they might the better know and judge of him and themselves.

But above all he excelled in prayer. The inwardness and weight of his spirit, the reverence and solemnity of his address and behaviour, and the fewness and fullness of his words have often struck even strangers with admiration, as they used to reach others with consolation. The most awful, living, reverent frame I ever felt or beheld, I must say, was his in prayer. And truly it was a testimony that he knew and lived nearer to the Lord than other men; for they that know him most will see most reason to approach him with reverence and fear.

He was of an innocent life, no busybody, nor self-seeker, neither touchy nor critical; what fell upon him was very inoffensive, if not very edifying. So meek, contented, modest, easy, steady, tender, it was a pleasure to be in his company. He exercised no authority but over evil, and that everywhere and in all, but with love, compassion, and long-suffering, a most merciful man, as ready to forgive as unapt to take or give an offence. Thousands can truly say he was of an excellent spirit and savour among them, and because thereof, the most excellent spirits loved him with an unfeigned and unfading love.

He was an incessant labourer; for in his younger time, before his many great and deep sufferings and travels had enfeebled his body for itinerant services, he laboured much in the word, and doctrine and discipline, in England, Scotland and Ireland, turning many to God, and confirming those that were convinced of the Truth, and settling good order as to church affairs among them.

I write by knowledge and not report; and my witness is true, having been with him for weeks and months together on divers occasions, and those of the nearest and most exercising nature, and that by night and by day, by sea and by land, in this and in foreign countries; and I can say I never saw him out of his place, or not a match for every service or occasion.

Civil beyond all forms of breeding, in his behaviour; very temperate, eating little and sleeping less, though a bulky person.

Thus he lived and sojourned among us; and as he lived, so he died; feeling the same eternal power, that had raised and preserved him, in his last moments. So full of assurance was he that he triumphed over death; and so even to the last, as if death were hardly worth notice or a mention.

I have done when I have left this short epitaph to his name. *Many sons have done virtuously in this day, but dear George thou excellest them all.*

—WILLIAM PENN

The Journal

1635

That all may know the dealings of the Lord with me, and the various exercises, trials, and troubles through which he led me.

I was born in the month called July in the year 1624, at Drayton-in-the-Clay in Leicestershire. My father's name was Christopher Fox; he was by profession a weaver, an honest man, and there was a Seed of God in him. The neighbours called him "Righteous Christer." My mother was an upright woman; her maiden name was Mary Lago, of the family of the Lagos and of the stock of the martyrs.

When I came to eleven years of age, I knew pureness and righteousness; for while I was a child I was taught how to walk to be kept pure. The Lord taught me to be faithful in all things, and to act faithfully two ways, viz., inwardly to God and outwardly to man, and to keep to "yea" and "nay" in all things. For the Lord showed me that though the people of the world have mouths full of deceit and changeable words, yet I was to keep to "yea" and "nay" in all things; and that my words should be few and savoury, seasoned with grace; and that I might not eat and drink to make myself wanton but for health, using the creatures in their service, as servants in their places, to the glory of him that hath created them.

Afterwards, as I grew up, my relations thought to have me a priest, but others persuaded to the contrary; whereupon I was put to a man, a shoemaker by trade, and that dealt in wool, and used grazing, and sold cattle; and a great deal went through my hands. While I was with him, he was blessed; but after I left him he broke, and came to nothing. I never wronged man or woman in all that time, for the Lord's power was with me and over me, to preserve me. While I was in that service, I used in my dealings the word "verily," and it was a common saying among people that knew me, "If George says 'Verily' there is no altering him." When boys and rude people would laugh at me, I let them alone and went my way, but people had generally a love to me for my innocency and honesty.

1644

Now during the time that I was at Barnet a strong temptation to despair came upon me. And then I saw how Christ was tempted, and mighty troubles I was in. And sometimes I kept myself retired in my chamber, and often walked solitary in the Chase there, to wait upon the Lord. And I wondered why these things should come to me; and I looked upon myself and said, "Was I ever so before?"

1646

When I was come down into Leicestershire, my relations would have had me married, but I told them I was but a lad, and I must get wisdom. Others would have had me into the auxiliary band among the soldiery, but I refused; and I was grieved that they proffered such things to me, being a tender youth. Then I went

to Coventry, where I took a chamber for a while at a professor's
house till people began to be acquainted with me, for there were
many tender people in that town.

And after some time I went into my own country again, and
was there about a year, in great sorrows and troubles, and walked
many nights by myself.

❧

I went to another ancient priest at Mancetter in Warwickshire
and reasoned with him about the ground of despair and temptations, but he was ignorant of my condition; and he bid me take
tobacco and sing psalms. Tobacco was a thing I did not love and
psalms I was not in an estate to sing; I could not sing. Then he
bid me come again and he would tell me many things, but when
I came again he was angry and pettish, for my former words had
displeased him.

1647

I brought them Scriptures, and told them there was an anointing
within man to teach him, and that the Lord would teach his people himself.

❧

About the beginning of the year 1647, I was moved of the Lord
to go into Derbyshire, where I met with some friendly people,
and had many discourses with them. Then passing further into
the Peak country, I met with more friendly people, and with
some in empty, high notions. And travelling on through some
parts of Leicestershire and into Nottinghamshire, there I met

with a tender people, and a very tender woman whose name was Elizabeth Hooton; and with these I had some meetings and discourses. But my troubles continued, and I was often under great temptations; and I fasted much, and walked abroad in solitary places many days, and often took my Bible and went and sat in hollow trees and lonesome places till night came on; and frequently in the night walked mournfully about by myself, for I was a man of sorrows in the times of the first workings of the Lord in me.

Oh, the everlasting love of God to my soul when I was in great distress! When my troubles and torments were great, then was his love exceeding great.

Now after I had received that opening from the Lord that to be bred at Oxford or Cambridge was not sufficient to fit a man to be a minister of Christ, I regarded the priests less, and looked more after the dissenting people. And among them I saw there was some tenderness, and many of them came afterwards to be convinced, for they had some openings. But as I had forsaken all the priests, so I left the separate preachers also, and those called the most experienced people; for I saw there was none among them all that could speak to my condition. And when all my hopes in them and in all men were gone, so that I had nothing outwardly to help me, nor could tell what to do, then, oh then, I heard a voice which said, "There is one, even Christ Jesus, that can speak to thy condition," and when I heard it my heart did leap for joy. Then the Lord did let me see why there was none upon the earth that could speak to my condition, namely, that I might give him all the glory; for all are concluded under sin, and shut up in unbelief as I had been, that Jesus Christ might have the pre-eminence, who enlightens, and gives grace, and faith and power. Thus, when God doth work who shall let [prevent] it? And this I knew experimentally.

And one day when I had been walking solitarily abroad and was come home, I was taken up in the love of God, so that I could not but admire the greatness of his love. And while I was in that condition it was opened unto me by the eternal Light and power, and I therein saw clearly that all was done and to be done in and by Christ, and how he conquers and destroys this tempter, the Devil and all his works, and is atop of him, and that all these troubles were good for me, and temptations for the trial of my faith which Christ had given me. And the Lord opened me that I saw through all these troubles and temptations. My living faith was raised, that I saw all was done by Christ, the life, and my belief was in him. And when at any time my condition was veiled, my secret belief was stayed firm, and hope underneath held me, as an anchor in the bottom of the sea, and anchored my immortal soul to its Bishop, causing it to swim above the sea, the world where all the raging waves, foul weather, tempests, and temptations are. But oh, then did I see my troubles, trials, and temptations more than ever I had done!

And therefore none can be a minister of Christ Jesus but in the eternal Spirit, which was before the Scriptures were given forth; for if they have not his Spirit, they are none of his.

Yet the work of the Lord went on in some, and my sorrows and troubles began to wear off and tears of joy dropped from me, so that I could have wept night and day with tears of joy to the Lord, in humility and brokenness of heart. And I saw into that which was without end, and things which cannot be uttered, and of the greatness and infiniteness of the love of God, which cannot be expressed by words. For I had been brought through the very ocean of darkness and death, and through the power and over the power of Satan, by the eternal glorious power of Christ. Even through that darkness was I brought, which covered over all the world, and which chained down all, and shut up all in death. And the same eternal power of God, which brought me through these things, was that which afterwards shook the nations, priests, professors, and people. Then could I say I had been in spiritual Babylon, Sodom, Egypt, and the grave; but by the eternal power of God I was come out of it, and was brought over it and the power of it, into the power of Christ. And I saw the harvest white, and the Seed of God lying thick in the ground, as ever did wheat that was sown outwardly, and none to gather it; and for this I mourned with tears.

1648

In the year 1648, as I was sitting in a Friend's house in Nottinghamshire (for by this time the power of God had opened the hearts of some to receive the word of life and reconciliation), I saw there was a great crack to go throughout the earth, and a great smoke to go as the crack went; and that after the crack there should be a great shaking. This was the earth in people's hearts, which was to be shaken before the Seed of God was raised out of the earth. And it was so; for the Lord's power began to shake them, and great meetings we began to have, and a mighty power and work of God there was amongst people, to the astonishment of both people and priests.

After this I went again to Mansfield, where was a great meeting of professors and people, and I was moved to pray, and the Lord's power was so great that the house seemed to be shaken. When I had done, some of the professors said it was now as in the days of the apostles, when the house was shaken where they were.

And at a certain time, when I was at Mansfield, there was a sitting of the justices about hiring of servants; and it was upon me from the Lord to go and speak to the justices that they should not oppress the servants in their wages. So I walked towards the inn where they sat but finding a company of fiddlers there, I did not go in but thought to come in the morning, when I might have a more serious opportunity to discourse with them, not thinking that a seasonable time. But when I came again in the morning, they were gone, and I was struck even blind that I could not see. And I inquired of the innkeeper where the justices were to sit that day and he told me at a town eight miles off. My

sight began to come to me again, and I went and ran thither-
ward as fast as I could. And then I was come to the house where
they were, and many servants with them, I exhorted the justices
not to oppress the servants in their wages, but to do that which
was right and just to them; and I exhorted the servants to do
their duties, and serve honestly, etc. And they all received my
exhortation kindly, for I was moved of the Lord therein.

Thus the work of the Lord went forward, and many were turned
from the darkness to the light within the compass of these three
years, 1646, 1647, and 1648. And divers meetings of Friends, in
several places, were then gathered to God's teaching, by his light,
spirit, and power; for the Lord's power brake forth more and
more wonderfully.

Now was I come up in spirit through the flaming sword into
the paradise of God. All things were new, and all the creation gave
another smell unto me than before, beyond what words can utter.
I knew nothing but pureness, and innocency, and righteousness,
being renewed up into the image of God by Christ Jesus, so that I
say I was come up to the state of Adam which he was in before he
fell. The creation was opened to me, and it was showed me how all
things had their names given them according to their nature and
virtue. And I was at a stand in my mind whether I should practise
physic for the good of mankind, seeing the nature and virtues of
the creatures were so opened to me by the Lord. But I was imme
diately taken up in spirit, to see into another or more steadfast state
than Adam's in innocency, even into a state in Christ Jesus, that

should never fall. And the Lord showed me that such as were faithful to him in the power and light of Christ should come up into that state in which Adam was before he fell, in which the admirable works of the creation, and the virtues thereof, may be known, through the openings of that divine Word of wisdom and power by which they were made. Great things did the Lord lead me into, and wonderful depths were opened unto me, beyond what can by words be declared; but as people come into subjection to the spirit of God, and grow up in the image and power of the Almighty, they may receive the Word of wisdom, that opens all things, and come to know the hidden unity in the Eternal Being.

I was to direct people to the Spirit that gave forth the Scriptures, by which they might be led into all Truth, and so up to Christ and God, as they had been who gave them forth.

These things I did not see by the help of man, nor by the letter, though they are written in the letter, but I saw them in the light of the Lord Jesus Christ, and by his immediate Spirit and power, as did the holy men of God, by whom the Holy Scriptures were written. Yet I had no slight esteem of the Holy Scriptures, but they were very precious to me, for I was in that spirit by which they were given forth, and what the Lord opened in me I afterwards found was agreeable to them.

Moreover when the Lord sent me forth into the world, he forbade me to put off my hat to any, high or low; and I was required to "thee" and "thou" all men and women, without any respect to rich or poor, great or small. And as I travelled up and down, I was not to bid people "good morrow" or "good evening," neither might I bow or scrape with my leg to any one; and this made the sects and professions to rage. But the Lord's power carried me over all to his glory, and many came to be turned to God in a little time, for the heavenly day of the Lord sprang from on high, and brake forth apace by the light of which many came to see where they were.

1649

Oh, the rage and scorn, the heat and fury that arose! Oh, the blows, punchings, beatings, and imprisonments that we underwent for not putting off our hats to men! For that soon tried all men's patience and sobriety, what it was. Some had their hats violently plucked off and thrown away so that they quite lost them. The bad language and evil usage we received on this account are hard to be expressed, besides the danger we were sometimes in of losing our lives for this matter, and that, by the great professors of Christianity, who thereby discovered that they were not true believers. And though it was but a small thing in the eye of man, yet a wonderful confusion it brought among all professors and priests. But, blessed be the Lord, many came to see the vanity of that custom of putting off the hat to men, and felt the weight of Truth's testimony against it.

Now after I was set at liberty from Nottingham gaol, where I had been kept prisoner a pretty long time, I travelled as before in the work of the Lord. And coming to Mansfield-Woodhouse, there was a distracted woman under a doctor's hand, with her hair loose all about her ears. He was about to let her blood, she being first bound, and many people being about her holding her by violence; but he could get no blood from her. And I desired them to unbind her and let her alone, for they could not touch the spirit in her, by which she was tormented. So they did unbind her; and I was moved to speak to her in the name of the Lord to bid her be quiet and still, and she was so. The Lord's power settled her mind, and she mended and afterwards received the Truth, and continued in it to her death. And the Lord's name was honoured, to whom the glory of all his works belongs.

Now while I was at Mansfield-Woodhouse, I was moved to go to the steeplehouse there on a First-day, out of the meeting in Mansfield, and when the priest had done I declared the Truth to the priest and people. But the people fell upon me with their fists, books, and without compassion or mercy beat me down in the steeplehouse and almost smothered me in it, being under them. And sorely was I bruised in the steeplehouse, and they threw me against the walls and when that they had thrust and thrown me out of the steeplehouse, when I came into the yard I fell down, being so sorely bruised and beat among them. And I got up again and then they punched and thrust and struck me up and down and they set me in the stocks and brought a whip to whip me, but did not. And as I sat in the stocks they threw stones at me, and my head, arms, breast, shoulders, back, and sides were so bruised that I was mazed and dazzled with the blows. And I was hot when they put me in the stocks. After some time they had me before the magistrate, at a knight's house and examined me, where were many great persons, and I reasoned with them of the things of God and his teachings, and Christ's, and how that God that made the world did not dwell in temples made with hands; and of divers things of the Truth I spake to them, and they, seeing how evilly I had been used, set me at liberty. The rude people were ready to fall upon me with staves but the constable kept them off. And when they had set me at liberty, they threatened me with pistols, if ever I came again they would kill me and shoot me; and they would carry their pistols to the steeplehouse. And with threatening I was freed. And I was scarce able to go or well to stand, by reason of ill-usage. Yet with much ado I got about a mile from the town, and as I was passing along the fields Friends met me. I was so bruised that I could not turn in my bed, and bruised inwardly at my heart, but after a while the power of the Lord went through me and healed me, that I was well, glory be to the Lord for ever.

From Coventry I went to a place called Atherstone, and when I was two miles off it the bell rang upon a market day for a lecture, and it struck at my life, and I was moved to go to the steeplehouse. And when I came into it I found a man speaking, and as I stood among the people the glory and life shined over all, and with it I was crowned. And when the priest had done I spoke to him and the people the truth and the light which let them see all that ever they had done, and of their teacher within them, and how the Lord was come to teach them himself, and of the Seed Christ in them; how they were to mind that, and the promise that was to the Seed of God within them, which is Christ.

And as I was passing on Leicestershire I came to Twycross, where there were excise-men, and I was moved of the Lord to go to them and warn them to take heed of oppressing the poor, and people were much affected with it. Now there was in that town a great man, that had long lain sick and was given over by the physicians; and some Friends in the town desired me to go to see him. And I went up to him and was moved to pray by him; spoke to him in his bed, and the power of the Lord entered him that he was loving and tender.

And I left him and came down among the family in the house, and spake a few words to the people that they should fear the Lord and repent and prize their time and the like words, and there came one of his servants with a naked sword and run at me ere I was aware of him, and set it to my side, and there held it, and I looked up at him in his face and said to him, "Alack for thee, it's no more to me than a straw." And then he went away in a rage, with threatening words, and I passed away [left town], and the power of the Lord came over all, and his master mended, according to my belief and faith that I had seen before. And he then turned this man away that run at me with the sword, and afterwards he was very loving to Friends; and when I came to that town again both he and his wife came to see me.

1650

There came an officer to me and took me by the hand and said I must go before the magistrates, and the other two that were with me, and so when we came before them about the first hour afternoon, they asked me why we came thither. I said God moved us to do so.

They put me in and out of the room from the first hour to the ninth hour at night in examinations, having me backward and forward, and said in a deriding manner that I was taken up in raptures, as they called it.

At last they asked me whether I was sanctified. I said, "Sanctified? yes," for I was in the paradise of God.

They said, had I no sin?

"Sin?" said I, "Christ my Saviour hath taken away my sin, and in him there is no sin."

They asked how we knew that Christ did abide in us.

I said, "By his Spirit that he has given us."

They temptingly asked if any of us were Christ.

I answered, "Nay, we are nothing. Christ is all."

They said, "If a man steal is it no sin?"

I answered, "All unrighteousness is sin."

And many such like words they had with me. And so they committed me as a blasphemer and as a man that had no sin, and committed another man with me to the House of Correction in Derby for six months.

This was Justice Bennet of Derby that first called us Quakers because we bid them tremble at the word of God, and this was in the year 1650. And the justices gave leave that I should have liberty to go a mile. And I perceived their end, and I told the gaoler that if they would set me how far a mile was, I might walk in it sometimes, but it's like they thought I would go away. I told them I was not of that spirit; and the gaoler confessed it after, that they did it with that intent to have me gone away to ease the plague from them, and they said I was an honest man.

And when I was in the House of Correction my relations came to me and were much troubled that I should be in prison, for they looked upon it to be a great shame to them for me to be in gaol. It was a strange thing to be imprisoned then for religion. They went to the justice that cast me into prison, and would have been bound in one hundred pounds; and others in Derby, fifty pounds apiece, that I might have gone home with them and that I should come no more amongst them to declare against the priests. They had me up before the justice with them; and because I would not have them to be bound, for I was innocent from any ill behaviour and had spoken the word of life and Truth unto them, Justice Bennet got up into a rage; and as I was kneeling down to pray to the Lord to forgive him, he ran upon me with both his hands and struck me and cried, "Away with him, gaoler. Take him away, gaoler." And some thought I was mad because I stood for purity, perfection, and righteousness.

1651

And when I was in the House of Correction, there came a trooper to me and said, as he was sitting in the steeplehouse hearing the priest he was in an exceeding great trouble and the voice of the Lord came to him saying, "What, dost not thou know that my servant is in prison? Go to him for directions." And he came, and I spake to his condition and opened his understanding, and settled his mind in the light and spirit of God in himself; and I told him that which showed him his sin and troubled him, for it would show him his salvation; for he that shows a man his sins is he that takes it away. So the Lord's power opened to him, so that he began to have great understanding of the Lord's Truth and mercies, and began to speak boldly in his quarters amongst the soldiers and others concerning Truth.

My time being nearly out of being committed six months to the House of Correction, they filled the House of Correction with persons that they had taken up to be soldiers [during April 1651, the Commonwealth forces were actively strengthened, following the discovery of a Royalist plot] and then they would have had me to be a captain of them and the soldiers cried they would have none but me. So the keeper of the House of Correction was commanded to bring me up before the Commissioners and soldiers in the market place; and there they proffered me that preferment because of my virtue as they said, with many other compliments, and asked me if I would not take up arms for the Commonwealth against the King. But I told them I lived in the virtue of that life and power that took away the occasion of all wars, and I knew from whence all wars did rise, from the lust according to James's doctrine. Still they courted me to accept of their offer and thought that I did but compliment with them. But I told them I was come into the covenant of peace which was before wars and strifes were. And they said they offered it in love and kindness to me because of my virtue, and such like flattering words they used, and I told them if that were their love and kindness I trampled it under my feet. Then their rage got up and they said, "Take him away, gaoler, and cast him into the dungeon amongst the rogues and felons"; which they then did and put me into the dungeon amongst thirty felons in a lousy, stinking low place in the ground without any bed. Here they kept me a close prisoner almost a half year, unless it were at times; and sometimes they would let me walk in the garden, for they had a belief of me that I would not go away.

And in this time I was exceeding much oppressed with judges and magistrates and courts, and was moved to write to the judges concerning their putting men to death for cattle and for money and small things, several times, how contrary to the law of God it was. One time, I was under great sufferings in my spirit through it, and under the very sense of death; but when I came out of it, standing in the will of God a heavenly breathing arose in my soul to the Lord. Then did I see the heavens opened and the glory of God shined over all. Two men suffered [were hanged] for small things, and I was moved to admonish them for their theft and encourage them concerning their suffering, it being contrary to the law of God; and a little after they had suffered their spirits appeared to me as I was walking, and I saw the men were well.

And there was a young woman that was to be put to death for robbing her master; and judgment was given and a grave made for her and she carried to execution. I was made to write to the Judge and to the jury about her, and when she came there though they had her upon the ladder with a cloth bound over her face, ready to be turned off, yet they had not power to hang her (as by the paper which I sent to be read at the gallows may be seen), but she was brought back again. And they came with great rage against me into the prison. Afterwards, in the prison this young woman came to be convinced of God's everlasting Truth.

So Worcester fight came on, and Justice Bennet sent the constables to press me for a soldier, seeing I would not accept of a command. I told them I was brought off from outward wars. They came down again to give me press-money but I would take none.

They offered me money twice, but I would not take it. Then they were wroth, and I was committed close prisoner without bail or mainprize. Thereupon I writ to them again, directing my letter to

Colonel Barton, who was a preacher, and the rest that were concerned in my commitment.

Now when they had gotten me into Derby dungeon, it was the belief and saying of people that I should never come out: but I had faith in God, and believed I should be delivered in his time; for the Lord had said to me before, that I was not to be removed from that place yet, being set there for a service which he had for me to do.

They could not agree what to do with me; and sometime they would have me up before the Parliament, and another time they would have banished me to Ireland. At first they called me a deceiver and seducer and a blasphemer; and then when God brought his plagues upon them they said I was an honest and virtuous man. But their good report and bad report, their well or ill speaking was nothing to me; for the one did not lift me up, nor the other cast me down, praised be the Lord.

At length they were made to turn me out of gaol about the beginning of winter in the year 1651, who had been kept a year, within three weeks, in four prisons, the House of Correction, and at the town prison and the county gaol and dungeon, and then in the high gaol where I was kept till I was set freely at liberty. And this was in the month called October in the Commonwealth's days. And then the light and truth and glory of the Lord flowed and spread abroad.

The next day I came to Cranswick to Captain Pursloe's. And he went with me to Justice Hotham's, a pretty tender man, that had some experience of God's working in his heart. After that I had some discourse with him of the things of God, he took me into his closet, and said he had known that principle this ten year, and he was glad that the Lord did now publish it abroad to people. And so after a while there came in a priest with whom I had some discourse concerning the Truth, but his mouth was quickly stopped, for he was nothing but a notionist, and not in possession of what he talked of.

And in the afternoon I went to the great high priest, their doctor, that Justice Hotham said he would send for to speak with me, to the steeplehouse three miles off, where he preached, and sat me down in the steeplehouse till the priest had done. And he took a text, which was, "Ho, every one that thirsteth, let him come freely, without money and without price." And so I was moved of the Lord God to say unto him, "Come down, thou deceiver and hireling, for dost thou bid people come freely and take of the water of life freely, and yet thou takest three hundred pounds off them for preaching the Scriptures to them. Mayest thou not blush for shame? Did the prophet Isaiah and Christ so do that spoke those words and gave them forth freely? Did not Christ command his ministers, 'Freely you have received, freely give'?" And so the priest, like a man amazed, packed away.

I came to a stack of hay and lay in the haystack all night in the snow and rain, being but three days before the time called Christmas.

I passed to Cleveland amongst those people that had tasted of the power of God, but were all shattered to pieces and the heads of them turned Ranters. Now they had had great meetings, so I told them after that they had had such meetings they did not wait upon God to feel his power to gather their minds together to feel his presence and power and therein to sit to wait upon him, for they had spoken themselves dry and had spent their portions and not lived in that which they spake, and now they were dry. They had some kind of meetings but took tobacco and drank ale in them and so grew light and loose.

1652

And a great deal of people gathered about me and I declared the Truth and the word of life to them. And after, I went to an inn and desired them to let me have a lodging and they would not; and I desired them to let me have a little meat and milk and I would pay them for it, but they would not.

And after I was passed a pretty way out of the town I came to another house and desired them to let me have a little meat and drink and lodging for my money, but they would not neither but denied me. And I came to another house and desired the same, but they refused me also; and then it grew so dark that I could not see the highway; but I discovered a ditch and got a little water and refreshed myself and got over the ditch and sat amongst the furze bushes, being weary with travelling, till it was day.

And I went to Gainsborough, and there, a Friend having been speaking in the market, the market and town were all in an uproar.

And in the eternal power of God I was moved of the Lord God to stand up atop of the table and tell them that Christ was in them except they were reprobates; and it was the eternal power of Christ and Christ that spake in me that time to them. And generally with one consent all the people did acknowledge the thing, and gave testimony to it, and confessed to it—yea, even the very professors and all them that were in a rage against me—and I said that if the power of God and the Seed spoke in man or woman it was Christ.

And the next First-day I went to Tickhill and there the Friends of that side gathered together and there was a meeting; and a mighty brokenness with the power of God there was amongst the people.

At night we came to a country house; and there being no ale-house near they desired us to stay there all night, where we had a good service for the Lord, declaring his Truth amongst them; for the Lord had said unto me if I did but set up one in the same spirit that the prophets and apostles were in that gave forth the Scriptures, he or she should shake all the country in their profession ten miles about them.

And the next day we passed on, warning people as we met them of the day of the Lord that was coming upon them. As we went I spied a great high hill called Pendle Hill, and I went on the top of it with much ado, it was so steep; but I was moved of the Lord to go atop of it; and when I came atop of it I saw Lancashire sea; and there atop of the hill I was moved to sound the day of the Lord; and the Lord let me see atop of the hill in what places he had a great people to be gathered. As I went down, on the hillside I found a spring of water and refreshed myself, for I had eaten little and drunk little for several days.

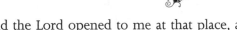

And the Lord opened to me at that place, and let me see a great people in white raiment by a river's side coming to the Lord.

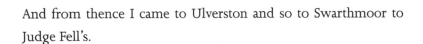

And from thence I came to Ulverston and so to Swarthmoor to Judge Fell's.

And so Margaret Fell had been abroad, and at night when she came home her children told her that priest Lampitt and I disagreed; and it struck something at her because she was in a profession with him, though he hid his dirty actions from them. So at night we had a great deal of reasoning and I declared the Truth to her and her family.

And the next day Lampitt came again and I had a great deal of discourse with him before Margaret Fell, who soon then discerned the priest clearly, and a convincement came upon her and her family of the Lord's Truth. And there was a humiliation day shortly after, within a day or two, kept at Ulverston, and Margaret Fell asked me to go to the steeplehouse with her, for she was not wholly come off. I said, "I must do as I am ordered by the Lord," so I left her and walked into the fields, and then the word of the Lord came to me to go to the steeplehouse.

Then I showed them that God was come to teach his people by his spirit and to bring them off all their old ways, religions, churches, and worship, for all their religions, and worship, and ways were but talking of other men's words, for they were out of the life and spirit that they were in that gave them forth.

One Justice Sawrey cried out, "Take him away"; and Judge Fell's wife said to the officers, "Let him alone, why may not he speak as well as any other."

I returned to Swarthmoor again, where the Lord's power seized upon Margaret Fell and her daughter Sarah and several of them.

And after this Judge Fell was come home, and Margaret sent for me to return thither, and so I came through the country back to Swarthmoor again; and the priests and professors, and that envious Justice Sawrey, had incensed Judge Fell and Captain Sandys much against the Truth with their lies; and after dinner I answered him all his objections and satisfied him by Scripture so as he was thoroughly satisfied and convinced in his judgment.

After we had discoursed a pretty time together, Judge Fell was satisfied that I was the man; and he came also to see by the spirit of God in his heart over all the priests and teachers of the world and did not go to hear them for some years before he died; for he knew it was the Truth, and that Christ was the teacher of his people and their saviour.

Richard Farnsworth and James Nayler were come to Swarthmoor also to see me and the family. (And James Nayler was under a fast fourteen days.) And Judge Fell, for all the opposition, let the meeting be kept at his house and a great meeting was settled there in the Lord's power to the tormenting of the priests and professors (which has remained above twenty years to this day), he being satisfied of the Truth. After I had stayed awhile and the meeting was settled, I went to Underbarrow and had a great meeting there and from thence to Kellet, and had a great meeting at Robert Widders's and many were convinced there, where several came from Lancaster and some from York.

And there was a captain stood up after the meeting was done and asked me where my leather breeches were, and I let the man run on awhile and at last I held up my coat and said, "Here are my leather breeches which frighten all your priests and professors."

And Margaret Fell had a vision of a man in a white hat that should come and confound the priests, before my coming into those parts.

And a man had a vision of me that a man in leather breeches should come and confound the priests, and this man's priest was the first that was confounded and convinced. And a great dread there was amongst the priests and professors concerning the man in leather breeches.

And after, I came up to Swarthmoor again, and there came up four or five priests, and I asked them whether any of them could say they ever had a word from the Lord to go and speak to such or such a people and none of them durst say so. But one of them burst out into a passion and said he could speak his experiences as well as I; but I told him experience was one thing but to go with a message and a word from the Lord as the prophets and the apostles had and did, as I had done to them, this was another thing.

Could any of them say they had such a command or word from the Lord at any time? But none of them could answer to it. But I told them the false prophets and false apostles and anti-christs could use the words and speak of other men's experiences that never knew or heard the voice of God and Christ; and such as they might get the good words and experience of others. This puzzled them much and laid them open.

About this time, 1652, Christopher Taylor, another minister, Thomas Taylor's brother, was convinced also of Truth; and they both became ministers of the gospel and great sufferers they were; and they came to know the word of the Lord and were commanded to go to many steeplehouses and markets and places and preach Christ freely. Also John Audland and Francis Howgill and John Camm came forth to be faithful ministers, and Edward Burrough, and Richard Hubberthorne, and Miles and Stephen Hubbersty and Miles Halhead and several others, and so continued till their deaths, and multitudes were turned to the Lord.

And James Nayler travelled up and down in many places amongst the people that were convinced. At last he and Francis Howgill were cast into Appleby gaol by the malicious priests and magistrates. And Francis Howgill and Edward Burrough died prisoners for the Lord's Truth.

They fell so upon Friends in many places that they could hardly pass the highways, stoning and beating and breaking their heads. And then the priests began to prophesy again that within a half year we should be all put down and gone.

And about a fortnight after, I went into Walney Island and James Nayler went with me and we stayed overnight at a little town on this side called Cocken, and had a meeting where there was one convinced. And in the evening there came a man who bound himself with an oath that he would shoot me with a pistol, many people being in the fold. And the people of the house went forth. And after a while I walked forth, the power of the Lord was so mighty to the chaining of them in the yard that the man of the house, being a professor, was so tormented and terrified that he went into a cellar to his prayers. And after I went into the house when Truth was come over them. And there was a raw man of the house, seeing the Truth had come over, he fell to speaking and let up their spirits. And so I walked out of the house into the yard again and fell a-speaking; and then the fellow drew his pistol. And he snapped his pistol at me but it would not go off, though he struck fire. And some held him and some carried me away, and so through the power of the Lord God I escaped. So the Lord's power came over them all, though there was a great rage in the country.

And Justice Sawrey and Justice Thompson of Lancaster granted forth a warrant for me, but Judge Fell, coming home, they did not serve it upon me, for he was out of the country all this time that I was thus abused and cruelly used.

And Judge Fell asked me to give him a relation of my persecution and I told him they could do not otherwise, they were in such a spirit; and they manifested their priests' fruits and profession and religion. So he told his wife that I made nothing of it and spoke as a man that had not been concerned; for the Lord's power healed me again.

And after this I went to Lancaster with Judge Fell to the Sessions where John Sawrey aforesaid, and Justice Thompson had given forth a warrant to apprehend me.

So I appeared at the Sessions upon the hearing of it, but was never apprehended by it. And there I met Colonel West, another justice.

And Colonel West stood up who had long been weak, and blessed the Lord and said he never saw so many sober people

and good faces together all the days of his life. He said that the
Lord had healed him that day, for he had been sick, and he said,
"George, if thou hast anything to say to the people, thou mayest
freely declare it in the open Sessions." So I was moved of the
Lord to speak, and as soon as I began, priest Marshall, their ora-
tor, goes his ways. And this I was moved to declare, that the
Scriptures were given forth by the spirit of God and all people
must first come to the spirit of God in themselves by which they
might know God and Christ, of whom the prophets and the
apostles learnt; and by the same spirit they might know the holy
Scriptures and the spirit which was in them that gave them
forth; so that spirit of God must be in them that come to know
them again, but which spirit they might have fellowship with
the Son and the Father and with the Scriptures and one with
another, and without it they cannot know neither God, nor
Christ, nor the Scriptures, nor have fellowship one with another.

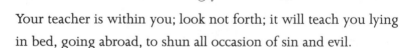

Your teacher is within you; look not forth; it will teach you lying
in bed, going abroad, to shun all occasion of sin and evil.

1653

And so after a while I visited many meetings in Lancashire, and
so came back to Swarthmoor again.

And then James Milner and Richard Myers went out into
imaginations [departed from the truth]. And a company followed
them. And I was in a fast about ten days, my spirit being greatly
exercised on Truth's account. And as Judge Fell and Colonel

Benson were in Swarthmoor Hall talking of the news in the News Book, of Parliament, etc., I was moved to tell them that before that day fortnight the Long Parliament should be broken up and the Speaker plucked out of his chair. And that day fortnight Colonel Benson came again and was speaking to Judge Fell and said that now he saw that George was a true prophet; for Oliver had broken up the Parliament by that time. And many openings I had of several things which would be too large to utter.

And great threatenings there were in Cumberland that if ever I came there they would take away my life; but when I heard of it I went into Cumberland to one Miles Wennington into the same parish but they had not power to touch me.

And also about this time Anthony Pearson, a great persecutor of Friends, was convinced at Appleby, over whose head they carried a sword when he went to the Bench. And coming over to Swarthmoor, I being at Colonel West's they sent for me and Colonel West said, "Go, George, for it may be of great service to the man"; and the Lord's power reached him.

So I called all people to the true teacher, out of the hirelings such as teach for the fleece and make a prey upon the people, for the Lord was come to teach his people himself by his spirit, and Christ saith, "Learn of me; I am the way" which doth enlighten every man that cometh into the world, that all through him might believe: and so to learn of him who had enlightened them, who was the Light.

And I brought them all to the spirit of God in themselves, by which they might know God and Christ and the Scriptures and to have heavenly fellowship in the Spirit; now the everlasting Gospel was preached again that brought life and immortality to light, and the day of the Lord was come, and Christ was come to teach his people himself and how they might find their teacher within, when they were in their labours and in their beds.

The Lord had given me a spirit of discerning by which I many times saw the states and conditions of people, and would try their spirits.

And the next day we came through that country into Cumberland again where we had a general meeting of many thousands of people atop of a hill, near Langlands. Heavenly and glorious it was and the glory of the Lord did shine over all, and there were as many as one could well speak over, there was such a multitude. Their eyes were kept to Christ their teacher and they came to sit under their vine, that afterwards a Friend in the ministry, Francis Howgill, went amongst them, and when he was moved to stand up amongst them he saw they had no need of words for they was all sitting down under their teacher Christ Jesus; so he was moved to sit down again amongst them without speaking anything.

So great a convincement there was in Cumberland, Bishoprick, Northumberland, Yorkshire, Westmorland, and Lancashire, and the plants of God grew and flourished so by heavenly rain, and God's glory shined upon them, that many mouths the Lord opened to his praise, yea to babes and sucklings he ordained strength.

But at the first convincement, when Friends could not put off their hats to people nor say "you" to a particular, but "thee" and "thou"; and could not bow nor use the world's salutations, nor fashions, nor customs, many Friends, being tradesmen of several sorts lost their custom at the first; for the people would not trade with them nor trust them, and for a time Friends that were tradesmen could hardly get enough money to buy bread. But afterwards people came to see Friends' honesty and truthfulness and "yea" and "nay" at a word in their dealing, and their lives and conversations did preach and reach to the witness of God in all people, and they knew and saw that for conscience sake towards God, they would not cozen and cheat them, and at last that they might send any child and be as well used as themselves, at any of their shops.

So then things altered so that all the enquiry was, where was a draper or shopkeeper or tailor or shoemaker or any other trades-man that was a Quaker; insomuch that Friends had double the trade, beyond any of their neighbours. And if there was any trad-ing they had it, insomuch that then the cry of all the professors and others was "If we let these people alone they will take the trading of the nation out of our hands."

1654

And so when the churches were settled in the north, the Lord had raised up many and sent forth many into his vineyard to preach his everlasting Gospel, as Francis Howgill and Edward

Burrough to London, John Camm and John Audland to Bristol through the countries, Richard Hubberthorne and George White-head towards Norwich, and Thomas Holme into Wales, a matter of seventy ministers did the Lord raise up and send abroad out of the north countries.

All Friends be low, and keep in the life of God to keep you low.

And so after I had visited the churches in the north and all were settled under God's teaching, and the glory of the Lord shined over them, I passed from Swarthmoor to Lancaster, and so through many towns, and felt I answered the witness of God in all people, though I spoke not a word. So I left the north fresh and green under Christ their teacher. And I came up into Yorkshire.

I was preserved in the everlasting Seed that never fell nor changes.

1655

And after I went to Leicester, and from Leicester to Whetstone; and before the meeting began there came a matter of seventeen troopers of Colonel Hacker's regiment with his marshall, and they took me up before the meeting.

Colonel Hacker asked me again if I would go home and stay at home; I told him if I should promise him so, that would manifest that I was guilty of something, for to go home and make my

home a prison; and if I went to meetings they would say I brake
their order; but I told them I should go to meetings as the Lord
ordered me, and therefore could not submit to that, but said we
were a peaceable people.

"Well then," said Colonel Hacker, "I will send you tomorrow
by six o'clock to my Lord Protector by Captain Drury, one of his
life-guard."

And when I was at London he left me at the Mermaid and went
and told Oliver Cromwell of me.

And I gave forth a paper and bid him carry it to Oliver, which
is here as followeth:

> *Dear Friend,*
> This is the word of the Lord God to thee. Live in
> the wisdom of the life of God, that with it thou
> mayest be ordered to his glory, and order his
> creatures to his glory. And be still and silent from
> thy own wisdom, wit, craft, subtilty, or policy
> that would arise in thee, but stand single to the
> Lord, without any end to thyself. Then God will
> bless thee and prosper thee in his ways; thou
> wilt feel his blessing in thy generation.
>
> And with thy mind stayed upon the Lord,
> thou wilt be kept in perfect peace, without any
> intent to thyself, to the glory of God. And there
> wilt thou feel no want, nor never a failing, nor
> forsaking, but the presence of the Lord God of
> life with thee. For now the state of this present

age is, that the Lord is bringing his people into
the life the Scriptures were given forth from, in
which life people shall come to have unity with
God, with Scriptures and one with another, for
the establishing righteousness, truth, and peace,
in which is the kingdom of God.

From a lover of thy soul and eternal good.
George Fox.

And after a few days I was had before Oliver Cromwell by Captain Drury.

Upon the Fifth-day of the First-month Captain Drury who
brought George Fox up to London by order from Colonel Hacker
did come to the inn into the chamber where George Fox lay and
said that it was required of George Fox from Oliver Cromwell
that he would promise that he would not take up a sword against
the Lord Protector or the Government as it is now; and that
George Fox would write down the words in answer to that which
the Protector required, and for George Fox to set his hand to it.

The Fifth-day of the First-month George Fox was moved of the
Lord to give out these words following which were given to
Oliver Cromwell. And George Fox was then presently brought
before him by Captain Drury.

George Fox to Oliver Cromwell, 1654 [1655 by
modern calendar]

I, who am of the world called George Fox, do
deny the carrying or drawing of any carnal

sword against any, or against thee, Oliver Cromwell, or any man. In the presence of the Lord God I declare it.

God is my witness, by whom I am moved to give this forth for the Truth's sake, from him whom the world calls George Fox; who is the son of God who is sent to stand a witness against all violence and against all the works of darkness, and to turn people from the darkness to the light, and to bring them from the occasion of the war and from the occasion of the magistrate's sword, which is a terror to the evil doers who act contrary to the light of the Lord Jesus Christ, which is a praise to them that do well, a protection to them that do well and not evil. Such soldiers as are put in that place no false accusers must be, no violence must do, but be content with their wages; and the magistrate bears not the sword in vain.

From under the occasion of that sword I do seek to bring people. My weapons are not carnal but spiritual, and "my kingdom is not of this world," therefore with a carnal weapon I do not fight, but am from those things dead; from him who is not of the world, called of the world by the name George Fox. And this I am ready to seal with my blood. . . .

From him who to all your souls is a friend, for establishing of rightcousness and cleansing the land of evil doers and a witness against all wicked inventions of men and murderous plots,

which answered shall be with the light in all
your consciences, which makes no covenant
with death, to which light in you all I speak,
and am clear.

G.F.

who is of the world called George Fox, who a
new name hath which the world knows not.

We are witnesses of this testimony, whose
names in the flesh are called
Thomas Aldam
Robert Craven

He brought me in before him before he was dressed, and one
Harvey (that had come amongst Friends but was disobedient)
waited upon him.

And so when I came before him I was moved to say, "Peace be
on this house"; and I bid him keep in the fear of God that he
might receive wisdom, that by it he might be ordered, that with
it he might order all things under his hand to God's glory. And I
spake much to him of Truth, and a great deal of discourse I had
with him about religion, wherein he carried himself very moder-
ately; but he said we quarrelled with the priests, whom he called
ministers.

And I told him the prophets, Christ, and the apostles declared
freely; and they declared against them that did not declare freely;

such as preached for filthy lucre and divined for money and preached for hire and were covetous and greedy like the dumb dogs that could never have enough; and such priests as did bear rule by their means and the people that loved to have it so. Now they that have the same spirit that Christ, and the prophets, and apostles had could not but declare against all such now as they did then. And several times he said it was very good, and truth, and I told him that all Christendom so called had the Scriptures but they wanted the power and spirit that they had that gave them forth; and therefore they were not in fellowship with the Son, nor with the Father, nor with the Scriptures, nor one with another.

And many more words I had with him. And many people began to come in, that I drew a little backward, and as I was turning he catched me by the hand and said these words with tears in his eyes, "Come again to my house; for if thou and I were but an hour in a day together we should be nearer one to the other," and that he wished me no more ill than he did to his own soul. And I told him if he did he wronged his own soul; and so I bid him hearken to and hear God's voice that he might stand in his counsel and obey it; if he did so, that would keep him from hardness of heart, and if he did not hear God's voice his heart would be hardened. And he said it was true. So I went out, and he bid me come again. And then Captain Drury came out after me and told me his Lord Protector said I was at liberty and might go whither I would, "And," says he, "my Lord says you are not a fool," and said he never saw such a paper in his life as I had sent him before by him. Then I was brought into a great hall, where the Protector's gentlemen were to dine; and I asked them what they did bring me thither for. They said, it was by the Protector's order, that I might dine with them. I bid them let the Protector know I would not eat a bit of his bread, nor drink a sup of his drink. When he heard this, he said that there was a people risen, meaning us, that he could not win either with honour, high places, nor gifts, but all other people he could. For we did not seek any of their places, gifts, nor honours, but their salvation and eternal good, both in this nation and elsewhere. But it was told him again that we had forsook our own, and were not like to look for such things from him.

The Lord's power went over the nation insomuch that many Friends were moved to go into most parts up and down the nation about this time, and into Scotland to sound forth the everlasting Gospel; and the glory of the Lord was set over all to his everlasting praise.

And a great convincement there was in London, and many in Oliver Protector's house and family.

And I went to see him again but could not get to him, the officers began to be so rude.

And sometimes they would turn up my coat and see for my leather breeches and then they would be in a rage.

Truth hath been talked of, but now it is possessed. Christ hath been talked of, but now he is come and is possessed.

What a world is this . . . they have lost the hidden man of the heart, and the meek and quiet spirit, which is of the Lord, of great price.

So the hearts of the people were opened by the spirit of God and they were turned from the hirelings to Christ Jesus their shepherd who had purchased them without money and would feed them without money or price. And Nicholas Beard and many others were convinced that day, that came to hear the dispute. And so the Lord's power came over all and his day many came to see. And abundance of Ranters and professors there were that had been so loose in their lives that they began to be weary of it and had thought to have gone into Scotland to have lived privately, and the Lord's Truth catched them all and their understandings were opened by his light, spirit, and power, through which they came to be settled upon the Lord; and so became very good Friends in the Truth and became very sober men, that great blessing and praising the Lord there was amongst them, and admiration in the country.

And after this I passed to Cambridge that evening, and when I came into the town it was all in an uproar, hearing of my coming, and the scholars were up, and were exceeding rude. But I kept on my horse-back and rid through them in the Lord's power. "Oh!" said they, "he shines, he glisters" but they unhorsed Captain Amor Stoddard before he could get to the inn;

and when we were in the inn they were exceeding rude in the
inn, and in the courts and in the streets. The miners, and colliers,
and cartmen could never be ruder.

And there John Crook met us at the inn. And the people of the
house asked me what I would have for supper, as is the usual way
of inns. "Supper," said I, "were it not that the Lord's power was
over these rude scholars it looked as if they would make a supper
of us and pluck us to pieces"; for they knew I was so against their
trade, which they were there as apprentices to learn, the trade of
preaching, that they raged as bad as ever Diana's craftsmen did
against Paul.

And this year came out the Oath of Abjuration from Oliver Protector, by which many Friends suffered. And several Friends went
to speak with him but he began to harden. And sufferings
increasing upon Friends by reason that envious magistrates made
use of that oath as a snare to catch Friends in, who they knew
could not swear at all.

God kept Friends over the rage of people; and great spoiling of
goods there was upon Friends for tithes by the Independent and
Presbyterian priests and some Baptist priests that had gotten into
steeplehouses, as the books of sufferings will declare. So I went
into Leicestershire where Colonel Hacker said if I came down
there he would imprison me again, though Oliver Protector had
set me at liberty; but I came down to Whetstone where his
troopers had taken me before; and Colonel Hacker's wife and his

marshall came to the meeting and were convinced. And the glorious, powerful day of the Lord was set over all, and many were convinced that day at that meeting, where were two Justices of Peace, Peter Price and Walter Jenkins, that came out of Wales, that were convinced and came to be ministers of Christ.

And they told me there were some Baptists and a Baptist woman sick, and John Rush went along to visit her. And when we came there were a-many people in the house that were tender about her; and they told me she was not a woman for this world, and if I had anything to comfort her concerning the world to come I might speak to her. So I was moved of the Lord God to speak to her and the Lord raised her up that she was well, to the astonishment of the town and country. Her husband's name was Baldock. And so we went to our inn again, and there were two desperate fellows fighting so that none durst come nigh them to part them, but I was moved in the Lord's power to go to them, and when I had loosed their hands, I held one by one hand and the other by the other hand; and I showed them the evil of their doings, and convinced them, and reconciled them each to other that they were loving and very thankful, so that people admired at it.

After awhile I went out of the city and left James Nayler behind me in London. And as I parted from him I cast my eyes upon him, and a fear struck in me concerning him.

1656

And from thence we passed into Cornwall, a dark country, through many desperate services and great opposition, but through the power of the Lord we came over all.

About this time I was moved to give forth the following exhortation to Friends in the ministry:

. . . Be patterns, be examples in all countries, places, islands, nations, wherever you come; that your carriage and life may preach among all sorts of people, and to them. Then you will come to walk cheerfully over the world, answering that of God in every one; whereby in them ye may be a blessing, and make the witness of God in them to bless you. Then to the Lord God you will be a sweet savour and a blessing.

And when I was in prison in Cornwall there was a Friend went to Oliver Cromwell and offered his body to him for to go to lie in Doomsdale prison for me or in my stead, that he would take him and let me go at liberty, and it so struck him and came over him that he said to his great men and his Council, "Which of you would do so much for me if I was in the same condition?"

And from Launceston we came through the countries to Exeter, where many Friends were in prison, and amongst the rest James Nayler, for a little before the time we were set at liberty, James ran out into imaginations, and a company with him; and they raised up a great darkness in the nation.

That night that we came to Exeter, I spoke with James Nayler, for I saw he was out and wrong and so was his company.

[Shortly after Fox's unhappy visit with Nayler in which Fox sensed that he "ran out into imaginations and a company with him," Nayler was released from Exeter prison and traveled to Bristol. The 1656 Nayler incident in Bristol, although ever so sketchily dealt with in Fox's Journal, was a major crisis both for the young and vulnerable Society of Friends and for Fox as its guide. Urged on by a number of adoring women followers, James Nayler had ridden into Bristol with his companions singing "Holy, Holy, Holy, Lord God of Israel" and flinging their cloaks in the mire for his horse to walk on, symbolizing the coming of Christ into Jerusalem. Nayler was arrested together with his companions, and while the companions were later released, Nayler was kept in prison and charged with blasphemy. When tried, he staunchly denied "James Nayler to be Christ but said that Christ was in him." After a long trial in Parliament itself, Nayler was found to be guilty of blasphemy. His cruel punishment included two public whippings across the city of London, with over 300 whip strokes each, and having his tongue bored through with a hot iron and his forehead branded with a B.

Next to George Fox, James Nayler had been, perhaps, the most effective voice in sharing the Quaker message, and this incident was a hard blow to the credibility of the Quaker witness. It confirmed the accusations of instability and illuminist fanaticism of which the enemies of the swiftly spreading Quaker movement had long accused it. In the course of Nayler's punishment, which he bore with the bravest of courage, he repented utterly and publicly of this incident and its effect in blunting the witness to his experience of Christ within, which he had given years of his life to proclaim.

George Fox had further distanced himself from James Nayler in the pain of this happening. The word of the London Yearly Meeting's Christian Faith and Practice on the outcome of this incident can scarcely be improved upon. "Having publicly abjured his follies in several statements, he sought to be reconciled with Fox who was lying ill and exhausted in Reading." Rebuffed, Nayler wrote to Margaret Fell: "My spirit was quieted in that simplicity in which I went, in that to return . . . and so His will is our peace." William Dewsbury was at last instrumental in bringing about a reconciliation between Nayler and Fox, and Nayler resumed his Quaker service, "living in great self-denial and very jealous of himself."

Out of this brokenness came such a sense of God's forgiveness and of humility and tenderness that the closing years of his life have touched Friends to the core. Once again, the above source tells of the final scene of his life and quotes a saying of Nayler's that is especially precious to Friends and that follows this statement: "In 1660 he set out on foot for the North, intending to go home to his wife and children. He was seen by a friend of Hertford, sitting by the wayside in meditation; and passed on through Huntingdon, where another friend saw him in such an awful frame as if he had been redeemed from the earth and a stranger on it, seeking a better country and inheritance. Some miles beyond Huntingdon, he was robbed and bound, and found towards evening in a field. He was taken to a Friend's house near King's Ripton, and passed away in the peace of God towards the end of October, 1660."

James Nayler's last words, spoken about two hours before his departure out of this life were:

There is a spirit which I feel that delights to do no evil, nor to revenge any wrong, but delights to endure all things, in hope to enjoy its own in the end. Its hope is to outlive all wrath and contention, and to weary out all exaltation and cruelty, or whatever is of a nature contrary to itself. It sees to the end of all temptations. As it bears no evil in itself, so it conceives none in thoughts to any other. If it be betrayed, it bears it, for its ground and spring is the mercies and forgiveness of God. Its crown is meekness, its life is everlasting love unfeigned; it takes its kingdom with entreaty and not with contention, and keeps it by lowliness of mind. In God alone it can rejoice, though none else regard it, or can own its life. It is conceived in sorrow, and brought forth without any to pity it, nor doth it murmur at grief and oppression. It never rejoiceth but through sufferings; for with the world's joy it is murdered. I found it alone, being forsaken. I have fellowship therein with them who lived in dens and desolate places in the earth, who through death obtained this resurrection and eternal holy life.]

And from thence (Exeter) we came to Bristol the Seventh-day night, to Edward Pyott's house, and it was noised over the town that I was come; and I had never been there before. And on the First-day morning I went to the meeting in Broadmead, and a great meeting there was, and quiet. And in the afternoon notice was given of a meeting to be in the orchard.

And so for many hours did I declare the word of life amongst them in the eternal power of God that by him they might come up into the beginning and be reconciled to God. And I showed them the types and figures and shadows of Christ in the time of the law, and showed them how that Christ was come that ended the types and shadows, and tithes and oaths, and denied swearing and set up "yea" and "nay" instead of it, and a free teaching. And now he was come to teach people himself, and how that his heavenly day was springing from on high. And I was moved to pray in the mighty power of the Lord and the Lord's power came over all.

And from thence we passed to London, and when we came near Hyde Park we saw a great clutter of people. And we espied Oliver Protector coming in his coach, and I rid up to his coach-side. But some of his life-guard would have put me away, but he forbade them. So I rid down by his coach-side with him declaring what the Lord gave me to say unto him of his condition, and of the sufferings of Friends in the nation, and how contrary this persecution was to Christ and to the apostles and Christianity. And I rid by his coach till we came to [St.] James Park gate, and he desired me to come to his house.

And the next day one of Oliver's wife's maids, Mary Saunders, came up to me to my lodgings and said that her master came to her and said he could tell her some good news. And she asked him what it was, if it were good that was well. And he said unto her George Fox was come to town: and she said that was good news indeed but could hardly believe it: but he told her how I met him and rid from Hyde Park down to James Park with him.

So the Lord's power came over all; and Friends were glad and the Lord had the glory and the praise.

And so Edward Pyott and I went to Whitehall after a time and when we came before him there was one Dr. John Owen, Vice-Chancellor of Oxford, with him; so we were moved to speak to Oliver Cromwell concerning the sufferings of Friends and laid them before him and turned him to the light of Christ who had enlightened every man that cometh into the world: and he said it was a natural light, and we showed him the contrary, and how it was divine and spiritual from Christ the spiritual and heavenly man, which was called the life in Christ, the Word and the light in us. And the power of the Lord God riz in me, and I was moved to bid him lay down his crown at the feet of Jesus.

And in this year 1656 the Lord's Truth was finely planted over this nation and many thousands were turned to the Lord; and seldom under a thousand in prison in the nation for tithes and going to the steeplehouses, and for contempts and not swearing and not putting off their hats. And Oliver Protector began to harden and several Friends were turned out of their offices of justices and other offices.

1657

And so I visited the meetings up and down in London; and some of them were troubled with rude people and apostates that had run out with James Nayler. And I was moved to write to Oliver Cromwell, and laid before him the sufferings of Friends in the nation and in Ireland.

And I was moved again to go and speak to Oliver Protector when there was a talk of making him King. And I met him in the Park and told him that they that would put on him an earthly crown would take away his life.

And he asked me, "What say you?"

And I said again, they that sought to put him on a crown would take away his life, and bid him mind the crown that was immortal.

And he thanked me after I had warned him of many dangers and how he would bring a shame and a ruin upon himself and

his posterity, and bid me go to his house. And then I was moved
to write to him and told him how he would ruin his family and
posterity and bring darkness upon the nation if he did so. And
several papers I was moved to write to him.

I had for some time felt drawings in my spirit to go into Scotland.

After some time we came to John Crook's house where a General
Yearly Meeting for the whole nation was appointed to be held.
This meeting lasted three days, and many Friends from most
parts of the nation came to it, so that the inns and towns around
were filled, for a matter of three or four thousand people were at
it. And although there was some disturbance by some rude people that had run out from Truth, yet the Lord's power came over
all, and a glorious meeting it was. The everlasting Gospel was
preached, and many received it, which brought life and immortality to light in them, and shined over all.

Then I was moved by the power and spirit of the Lord, to
open unto them the promise of God, how that it was made to
the Seed, not to seeds, as many, but to one, which Seed was
Christ; and that all people, both males and females, should feel
this Seed in them, which was heir of the promise; that so they
might all witness Christ in them, the hope of glory, the mystery
which had been hid from ages and generations, which was
revealed to the apostles, and is revealed again now, after this long
night of apostacy.

About this time she they called the Lady Claypole [Elizabeth Cromell] was very sick and troubled in mind, and nothing could comfort her. And I was moved of the Lord to write a paper and send it to her to be read unto her.

Friend,

Be still and cool in thy own mind and spirit from thy own thoughts, and then thou wilt feel the principle of God to turn thy mind to the Lord God, whereby thou wilt receive his strength and power from whence life comes, to allay all tempests, against blusterings and storms. That is it which moulds up into patience, into innocency, into soberness, into stillness, into stayedness, into quietness, up to God, with his power. . . .

Therefore be still a while from thy own thoughts, searching, seeking, desires and imaginations, and be stayed in the principle of God in thee, to stay thy mind upon God, up to God; and thou wilt find strength from him and find him to be a present help in time of trouble, in need, and to be a God at hand. And it will keep thee humble being come to the principle of God, which hath been transgressed; which humble, God will teach in his way, which is peace; and such he doth exalt. And now as the principle of God in thee hath been transgressed, come to it, to keep thy mind down low, up to the Lord God; and deny thyself. And from thy own will, that is, the earthly, thou must be kept. Then thou wilt feel the power of God, that will bring nature into his course, and to see the glory of the first body. And there the wisdom of God will be received, which is Christ, by which all things were made and created, in wisdom to be preserved and ordered to God's glory. There thou wilt come to receive and feel the physician of value, which clothes people in their right mind, whereby they may serve God and do his will. . . .

Looking down at sin, and corruption, and distraction, you are swallowed up in it; but looking at the light that discovers them, you will see over them. That will give victory; and you will find grace and strength; and there is the first step of peace. That will bring salvation; and see to the beginning and the glory that was with the Father before the world began; and so come to know the Seed of God which is heir of the promise of God, and the world which hath no end; unto the power of an endless life, which power of God is immortal, which brings up the soul, which is immortal, up to the immortal God, in whom it doth rejoice. So in the name and power of the Lord Jesus Christ, strengthen thee.

G.F.

And she said it settled and stayed her mind for the present. And many Friends got copies of it, both in England and Ireland, to read it to distracted people; and it settled several of their minds, and they did great service with it both in England and Ireland.

And many Friends being in prisons at this time, a matter of two hundred were moved to go to the Parliament to offer up themselves to lie in the same dungeons where their friends lay, that they that were in prison might go forth and not perish in the stinking dungeons and gaols. And this we did in love to God and our brethren that they might not die in prison, and in love to them that cast them in, that they might not bring innocent blood upon their own heads which would cry to the Lord, and bring his wrath and vengeance and plagues upon them.

And then the Parliaments would be in a rage and sometimes send them word that they would whip them and send them home again; and many times soon after the Lord would turn them out and send them home, who had not power to do good in their day. And when the Long Parliament sat I was moved to send several papers to them and speak to them how the Lord was bringing a day of darkness upon them all that should be felt.

One time, as I was going into the country, and two Friends with me, when I was gone a little above a mile out of the city, there met me two troopers who took me and the Friends that were with me prisoners and brought us to the Mews and there kept us. They were Colonel Hacker's men, but the Lord's power was so over them that they did not take us before any officers, but shortly after set us at liberty again.

And the same day, I took boat and went to Kingston, and from thence I went afterwards to Hampton Court, to speak with the Protector about the sufferings of Friends. I met him riding into Hampton-Court Park, and before I came at him he was riding in the head of his life-guard, I saw and felt a waft of death go forth against him, and he looked like a dead man. When I had spoken to him of the suffering of Friends and warned him as I was moved to speak to him, he bid me come to his house. So I went to Kingston, and the next day went up to Hampton Court. But when I came, he was very sick, and Harvey told me, who was one of his men that waited on him, that the doctors were not willing I should come in to speak with him. So I passed away, and never saw him no more.

From Kingston I went to Isaac Penington's, in Buckinghamshire, where I had appointed a meeting, and the Lord's truth and power came over all.

And after I had visited Friends in London and in the country thereaways I went into Essex. And there I had not been long before I heard Oliver Protector was dead. And then I came up to London again when Richard, his son, was made Protector.

And there was great persecution about seven miles off London. The rude people usually came out of several parishes so that they beat, abused, and bruised Friends exceedingly. And one day they beat and abused about eighty Friends that went out of London to a meeting, and tore their coats and cloaks off their backs and threw them into ditches and ponds, and all moiled them with dirt.

And great sufferings I had about this time; and great confusion and distraction there was amongst the powers and people.

And after a while I passed to Reading, and was under great sufferings and exercises, and in a great travail in my spirit for ten weeks' time. For I saw how the powers were plucking each other to pieces. And I saw how many men were destroying the simplicity and betraying the Truth. And a great deal of hypocrisy, deceit, and strife was got uppermost in people, that they were ready to sheath their swords in one another's bowels.

And this time, towards 1659, the powers had hardened themselves, persecuting Friends, and had many of them in prison, and were crucifying the Seed, Christ, both in themselves and others. And at last they fell a-biting and devouring one another until they were consumed one of another; who had turned against and judged that which God had wrought in them and showed them. So, God overthrew them, and turned them upside down, and brought the King over them, who were always complaining that the Quakers met together to bring in King Charles, whereas Friends did not concern themselves with the outward powers.

So when I had travailed with the witness of God which they had quenched, and I had gotten through with it and over all that hypocrisy, and saw how that would be turned under and down, and that life would rise over it, I came to have ease, and the light, power, and spirit shined over all. And in this day many of our old envious persecutors were in great confusion.

I had a sight and sense of the King's return a good while before, and so had some others. For I several times writ to Oliver Cromwell and told him, while he was persecuting God's people, those he looked upon as his enemies were preparing to come upon him. Several rash spirits would have bought Somerset House that we might have meetings in it, but I was moved of the Lord to forbid them so to do, for I did foresee the King's coming in again at that time.

1660

And great fears and troubles were in many people and a looking for the King Charles II coming in, and that all things should be altered; but I told them the Lord's power and light was over all and shined over all, and that the fear would only take hold of the hypocrites and such as had not been faithful to God, our persecutors. For in my travail and sufferings at Reading when people were at a stand and could not tell what might come in nor who might rule, I told them the Lord's power was over all, for I had travailed through it, and his day shined, whosoever should come in; and all would be well whether the King came in or no, to them that loved God and were faithful to him; and so I bid all Friends to fear none but the Lord, and keep in his power which is over all.

🦚

And I had a General Meeting at Edward Pyott's near Bristol where there were many thousands of people, for beside Friends from many parts thereabouts some of the Baptist and Independent teachers came to it and all was quiet, for most of the sober people came out of Bristol to it. And the people that stayed in the city said the city looked naked, the sober people were so gone forth to this meeting. And the Lord's everlasting Seed, Christ Jesus, was set over all that day.

And at this meeting some Friends did come out of most parts of the nation, for it was about business of the church both in this nation and beyond the seas. For when I was in the north, several years before, I was moved to set up that meeting, for many Friends suffered and their goods were spoiled wrongfully, contrary to the law. And so several Friends that had been justices and magistrates and that did understand the law came there and were able to inform Friends, and to gather up the sufferings that they might be laid before the justices and judges.

And justices and captains had come to break up this meeting, but when they saw Friends' books and accounts of collections concerning the poor, how that we did take care one county to help another, and to provide for our poor that none of them should be chargeable to their parishes, etc., and took care to help Friends beyond the seas, the justices and officers were made to confess that we did their work and Friends desired them to come and sit with them then.

And then they began to imprison and persecute Friends because that we would not give them tithes, and many thousands of our Friends in their days suffered imprisonments. And many thousand pounds worth of goods were taken away from them, so that they made many widows and fatherless, for many died in prison that they had caused to be cast into prison.

1661

Though Oliver Cromwell at Dunbar fight had promised to the Lord that if he gave him the victory over his enemies he would take away tithes or else let him be rolled into his grave with infamy, when the Lord had given his victory and he came to be chief, he confirmed the former laws that if people did not set forth their tithes they should pay treble, and this to be executed by two justices of peace in the country upon the oath of two witnesses.

There were about seven hundred Friends in prison in the nation, upon contempts to Oliver's and Richard's government; and when the King came in he set them all at liberty. It was said there was something drawn up that we should have our liberty, only it wanted signing. And then the Fifth-Monarchy people rose and a matter of thirty of them made an insurrection in London. On the First-day there were glorious meetings and the Lord's truth shined over all and his power was set over all. And at midnight, soon after, the drums beat and they cried, "Arms, arms!" which caused the trained bands and soldiers to arise, both in the city and country.

And I got up out of bed, and in the morning took boat and came down to Whitehall stairs and went through Whitehall; and they looked strangely upon me; and I went to the Pall Mall. And all the city and suburbs were up in arms and exceeding rude; all people were against us and they cried, "There is a Quaker's house, pluck it down." And divers Friends came thither to me; and as a Friend, one Henry Fell, was going to a General Meeting at Major Beard's, the soldiers knocked him down and he had been killed if the Duke of York had not come by. And all the prisons were soon after filled with Friends and many died in prison, they being so thronged up. And many inns were full, both in cities, towns, and country; and it was hard for any sober people to stir for several weeks' time.

Margaret Fell went to the King and told him what work there was in the city and nation and showed him that we were a peaceable innocent people and that we must keep our meetings as we used to do and that it concerned him to see that peace was kept, that so no blood might be shed.

And all the posts were laid open to search all letters, so that none could pass; but we heard of several thousands of our Friends that were cast into prison, and Margaret Fell carried the account to the King and Council. And the third day after we had an account of several thousands more that were cast into prison, and she went and laid them also before the King and his Council; and they wondered how we could have such intelligence, seeing they had given such strict charge for the intercepting all letters; but the Lord did so order it that we had an account as aforesaid, notwithstanding all their stoppings. And then we drew up another declaration and got it printed, and sent some of them to

the King and Council. And they were sold up and down the
streets and at the Exchange, which declaration is as followeth:

> This Declaration was given unto the King upon
> the 21st day of the 11th Month, 1660 [January
> 1661].
>
> *A Declaration from the harmless and innocent people of God,
> called Quakers, against all plotters and fighters in the world,*
> for the removing the ground of jealousy and
> suspicion from both magistrates and people in
> the kingdom, concerning wars and fightings.
> And also something in answer to that clause of
> the King's late Proclamation which mentions the
> Quakers, to clear them from the [Fifth Monar-
> chy] plot and the fighting which therein is
> mentioned, and for the clearing their
> innocency.
>
> Our principle is, and our practices have
> always been, to seek peace and ensue it and to
> follow after righteousness and the knowledge of
> God, seeking the good and welfare and doing
> that which tends to the peace of all. We know
> that wars and fightings proceed from the lusts of
> men (as Jas iv. 1–3), out of which lusts and the
> Lord hath redeemed us, and so out of the occa-
> sion of war. The occasion of which war, and war
> itself (wherein envious men, who are lovers of
> themselves more than lovers of God, lust, kill,
> and desire to have men's lives and estates)
> ariseth from the lust. All bloody principles and

practices, we, as to our own particulars, do utterly deny, with all outward wars and strife and fightings with outward weapons, for any end or under any pretence whatsoever. And this is our testimony to the whole world. . . .

That the spirit of Christ, by which we are guided, is not changeable, so as once to command us from a thing as evil and again to move unto it; and we do certainly know, and so testify to the world, that the spirit of Christ, which leads us into all Truth, will never move us to fight and war against any man with outward weapons, neither for the kingdom of Christ, nor for the kingdoms of this world. . . .

For this we can say to the whole world, we have wronged no man's person or possessions, we have used no force nor violence against any man, we have been found in no plots, nor guilty of sedition. When we have been wronged, we have not sought to revenge ourselves, we have not made resistance against authority, but wherein we could not obey for conscience' sake, we have suffered even the most of any people in the nation. We have been accounted as sheep for the slaughter, persecuted and despised, beaten, stoned, wounded, stocked, whipped, imprisoned, haled out of synagogues, cast into dungeons and noisome vaults where many have died in bonds, shut up from our friends, denied needful sustenance for many days together, with other the like cruelties.

And this is both our principle and practice, and hath been from the beginning, so that if we suffer, as suspected to take up arms or make war against any, it is without any ground from us; for it neither is, nor ever was in our hearts, since we owned the Truth of God; neither shall we ever do it, because it is contrary to the spirit of Christ, his doctrine, and the practice of his apostles, even contrary to him for whom we suffer all things, and endure all things.

And whereas men come against us with clubs, staves, drawn swords, pistols cocked, and do beat, cut and abuse us, yet we never resisted them, but to them our hair, backs, and cheeks have been ready. It is not an honour to manhood nor to nobility to run upon harmless people who lift not up a hand against them, with arms and weapons.

And there was a great darkness both in the city and country; but this declaration of ours cleared the air and laid the darkness, and the King gave forth after this a little proclamation that no soldiers should go to search any house but with a constable.

And at the execution of these Monarchy Men they cleared us from having any hand in their plot.

And after the light had shined over all, though many thousands were imprisoned up and down the nation, all gaols being full, the King gave forth after this a declaration that Friends should be set at liberty without paying fees. And so the

Truth, with great labour, travail, and care, came over all, for Margaret [Fell] and Thomas Moore went often to the King and he was tender towards them.

Friends, your sufferings, all that are or have been of late in prison, I would have you send up an account of them, how things are amongst you, which is to be delivered unto the King and his Council; for things are pretty well here after the storm.

Oh, the daily reproaches and beatings in highways because we would not put off our hats, and for saying "thou" to people; and the priests spoiling our goods because we could not put into their mouths and give them tithes, besides casting in prison as the records and books of sufferings testify, and besides the great fines in courts for not swearing. But with them for all these things the Lord God did plead.

And I was moved to write to those justices and to tell them did we ever resist them when they took our ploughs and plough-gear, our cows and horses, our corn and cattle, and kettles and platters from us, and whipped us, and set us in the stocks, and cast us in prison, and all this for serving and worshiping of God in spirit and truth and because we could not conform to their religions, manners, customs, and fashions. Did we ever resist them? Did we not give them our backs and our cheeks and our faces to spit on, and our hair to pluck at?

And before this time we received account from New England that they had made a law to banish the Quakers out of their colonies, upon pain of death in case they returned; and that several Friends, so banished, returning were taken and hanged, and that divers more were in prison, in danger of the like sentence. And when they were put to death, as I was in prison at Lancaster, I had a perfect sense of it, as though it had been myself, and as though the halter had been put about my neck.

But as soon as we heard of it, Edward Burrough went to the King, and told him there was a vein of innocent blood opened in his dominions, which, if it were not stopped, would overrun all. To which the King answered, "But I will stop that vein." Edward Burrough said, "Then do it speedily, for we do not know how many may soon be put to death." The King answered, "As speedily as ye will. Call," said he to some present, "the secretary, and I will do it presently." The secretary being called, a mandamus was forthwith granted. A day or two after, Edward Burrough going again to the King, to desire the matter might be expedited, the King said he had no occasion at present to send a ship thither, but if we would send one, we might do it as soon as we would. Edward Burrough then asked the King if it would please him to grant his deputation to one called a Quaker, to carry the mandamus to New England. He said, "Yes, to whom ye will." Whereupon Edward Burrough named one Samuel Shattuck (as I remember) who, being an inhabitant of New England, was banished by their law to be hanged if he came again; and to him the deputation was granted. Then we sent for one Ralph Goldsmith, an honest Friend, who was master of a good ship, and agreed with him for £300, goods or no goods, to sail in ten days. He forthwith prepared to set sail, and with a prosperous gale, in about six weeks time arrived before the town of Boston in New England upon a First-day morning, called Sunday. With him went many passengers, both of New and Old England, that were Friends whom the Lord did move to go to bear their testimony against those bloody persecutors, who had exceeded all the world in that age in their persecutions.

The townsmen at Boston, seeing a ship come into the bay with English colours, soon came on board, and asked for the captain. Ralph Goldsmith told them he was the commander. They asked him if he had any letters. He said, "Yes." They asked if he would deliver them. He said, "No, not to-day." So they went a-shore and reported there was a ship full of Quakers, and that Samuel Shattuck was among them, who they knew was, by their law, to be put to death for coming again after banishment; but they knew not his errand, nor his authority.

So all being kept close that day, and none of the ship's company suffered to land, next morning, Samuel Shattuck, the King's deputy, and Ralph Goldsmith, the commander of the vessel, went on shore; and sending back to the ship the men that landed them, they two went through the town to the governor John Endicott's door, and knocked. He sent out a man to know their business. They sent him word their business was from the King of England, and they would deliver their message to none but the governor himself. Thereupon they were admitted to go in,

and the governor came to them, and having received the deputation and the mandamus, he laid off his hat, and looked upon
them. Then going out, he bid the Friends follow him. So he went
to the deputy-governor, and after a short consultation, came out
to the Friends, and said, "We shall obey his Majesty's com-
mands," as by the order may be seen, and the relation in William
Coddington's book, who is governor of Rhode Island and a
Friend. After this, the master gave liberty to the passengers to
come on shore, and presently the noise of the business flew
about the town, and the Friends of the town and the passengers
of the ship met together to offer up their praises and thanksgiv-
ings to God, who had so wonderfully delivered them from the
teeth of the devourer. While they were thus met, in came a poor
Friend who, being sentenced by their bloody law to die, had lain
some time in irons, expecting execution. This added to their joy,
and caused them to lift up their hearts in high praises to God,
who is worthy for ever to have the praise, the glory, and the honour; for he only is able to deliver, and to save, and to support all
that sincerely put their trust in him.

1662

Now there being very many Friends in prison in the nation,
Richard Hubberthorne and I drew up a paper concerning them,
and got it delivered to the King, that he might understand how
we were dealt with by his officers.

1663

[*After word of Edward Burrough's death in prison, George Fox*] wrote the following lines for the staying and settling of Friends' minds;

> *Friends,*
> Be still and wait in your own conditions, and settled in the Seed of God that doth not change, that in that ye may feel dear Edward Burrough among you in the Seed, in which and by which he begat you to God, with whom he is; and that in the Seed ye may all see and feel him, in the which is unity in the life with him. And so enjoy him in the life that doth not change, but which is invisible.
> G.F.

1664

And after the meeting was done I came over the Sands to Swarthmoor.

And the next day a lieutenant of a foot company came with his sword and pistol to take me, and I told him I knew his message and errand the night before, and so had given up myself to be taken; for if I would have escaped their imprisonment I might have been forty miles off before they came; but I was an innocent man and so mattered not what they could do unto me.

And so I was kept in prison until the Assizes [a session of the court].

And when they and the jury were sworn, the judge asked me whether I had refused the oath, the last Assizes.

And I said that I never took oath in my life, and Christ the saviour and judge of the world saith, "Swear not at all."

The judge said you refused it [the oath] at the Assizes and I can tender the oath to any man now and praemunire him [have the government seize his property] for not taking it, and he said they might bring me in guilty, I denying the oath.

He spoke to the jury, and the jury brought in for the King, "Guilty."

So presently they set me aside, and Margaret Fell was called, who had a great deal of good service among them. Many more words were spoken concerning the Truth. And so the court broke up near the second hour.

And in the afternoon we were brought up to have our sentence passed upon us. And Margaret Fell desired that judgment and sentence might be deferred till the next morning.

Then the judge bid the gaoler take me away, and I was had away to my chamber and they passed away from the court. And the Truth and power of the Lord God was glorious over all. And many spirits were crossed grievously in their envy and malice. And Margaret Fell they praemunired, and he passed sentence upon her.

1665

And so they committed me again to close prison. And Colonel Kirby gave order to the gaoler that no flesh alive must come at me for I was not fit to be discoursed with by men.

So I was put up in a smoky tower where the smoke of the other rooms came up and stood as a dew upon the walls, where it rained in also upon my bed and the smoke was so thick as I could hardly see a candle sometimes, and many times I was locked under three locks; and the under-gaoler would hardly come up to unlock one of the upper doors; the smoke was so thick that I was almost smothered with smoke and so starved with cold and rain that my body was almost numbed, and my body swelled with the cold.

And many times when I went to stop out the rain off me in the cold winter season, my shift would be as wet as muck with rain that came in upon me. And as fast as I stopped it the wind, being high and fierce, would blow it out again; and in this manner did I lie all that long cold winter till the next Assizes.

And often they threatened to hang me over the wall and the officers often in their rage would bid the soldiers shoot me and run me through, and the deputy governor said that the King, knowing I had a great interest in the people, had sent me thither, that if any stir was in the nation they might hang me over the walls to keep the people down.

1666

But at last the governor came under some trouble having sent out a privateer who had taken some ships that were not enemies' ships but their friends and so came under trouble, after which he grew somewhat more friendly to me.

And I desired him when he came to London, he being a Parliament man, that he would speak to Esquire Marsh and to Sir Francis Cobb and some others, and tell them that I was a prisoner, and for what, and how long I had lain in prison, and he did so.

And when he came down again he told me that Esquire Marsh, that was one of the King's esquires of his body, said he would go one hundred miles barefoot for my liberty, he knew me so well, and that several others spoke well of me. So the governor was very loving to me.

And after a while John Whitehead brought an order from the King for my release.

And so after I had passed through many counties and had large meetings, visiting Friends and my relations, I came at last to London.

But I was so weak with lying about three years in cruel and hard imprisonments, my joints and my body were so stiff and benumbed that I could hardly get on my horse. Neither could I well bend my knees, nor hardly endure fire nor eat warm meat: I had been so long kept from it.

And so after I had visited Friends' meetings in London, which were large and precious, I walked into the ruins of the city that was burnt, which I saw lying according as the word of the Lord came to me concerning it several years before.

1667

Blessed be the Lord. And though I was very weak, yet I travelled up and down in the service of the Lord.

And then I was moved of the Lord God to set up and establish five Monthly Meetings of men and women in the city of London, besides the Women's Meeting and the Quarterly Meeting, to admonish, and exhort such as walked disorderly or carelessly, and not according to Truth; and to take care of God's glory.

And the Lord opened to me and let me see what I must do, and how I must order and establish the Men's and Women's Monthly and Quarterly Meetings in all the nation, and write to other nations, where I came not, to do the same.

1668

And as I was lying in my bed the word of the Lord came to me that I must go back to London. And Alexander Parker and several others came to me the next morning, and I asked them what they felt. And they asked me what was upon me, and I told them I felt I must return to London, and they said it was upon them the same. And so we gave up to return to London, for which way the Lord moved us and led us we went in his power.

Then I came to Waltham and established a school there for teaching of boys, and ordered a women's school to be set up at Shacklewell to instruct young lasses and maidens in whatsoever things were civil and useful in the creation.

1669

Now I was moved of the Lord to go over into Ireland, to visit the Seed of God in that nation.

When we came on shire in Ireland, the earth and the very air smelt with the corruption of the nation and gave another smell than England to me, with the corruption and the blood and the massacres and the foulness that ascended.

Now the Province of Munster's Meeting (to which General Meeting of Cork belongs) and Men's Meeting were over, wherein the power of the Lord was so great that Friends in the power and spirit of the Lord brake out into singing, many together with an audible voice making melody in their hearts; at this time I was moved to declare to Friends in the ministry.

I passed to other meetings, where the power of the Lord God and his spirit was wonderfully manifested to the refreshing of Friends, and from thence to the Foxe's country, who claimed kindred, but I told them that my kindred were they that stood in the life and power of God.

And a good, weighty people there is, and true, and tender, and sensible of the power of the Lord God, and his Truth in that nation (Ireland) worthy to be visited; and very good order they have in their meetings, and they stand up for righteousness and holiness, that dams up the way of wickedness. Oh, the sufferings and trials gone through, by reason of the bad spirits! The Lord have the glory, whose power went over them, like a tide that covers the earth.

And there [Bristol] Margaret Fell and her daughters and sons-in-law met me, where we were married. Margaret Fell was come to visit her daughter Yeamans.

I had seen from the Lord a considerable time before that I should take Margaret Fell to be my wife. And when I first mentioned it to her she felt the answer of life from God thereunto. But though the Lord had opened this thing unto me, yet I had not received a command from the Lord for the accomplishment of it then. Wherefore I let the thing rest, and went on in the work and service of the Lord as before, according as the Lord led me, travelling up and down in this nation and through the nation of Ireland. But now, after I was come back from Ireland and was come to Bristol and found Margaret Fell there, it opened in me from the Lord that the thing should be now accomplished.

And after we had discoursed the thing together I told her if she also was satisfied with the accomplishing of it now she should first send for her children, which she did. And when the rest of her daughters were come I was moved to ask the children and her sons-in-law whether they were all satisfied and whether Margaret had answered them according to her husband's will to her children, she being a widow, and if her husband had left anything to her for the assistance of her children, in which if she married they might suffer loss, whether she had answered them in lieu of that and all other things. And the children made answer and said she had doubled it, and would not have me to speak of those things. I told them I was plain and would have all things done plainly, for I sought not any outward advantage to myself.

And so when I had thus acquainted the children with it, and when it had been laid before several meetings both of the men and women, assembled together for that purpose, and all were satisfied, there was a large meeting appointed of purpose in the meeting-house at Broad Mead in Bristol, the Lord joining us together in the honourable marriage in the everlasting covenant and immortal Seed of life, where there were several large testimonies borne by Friends.

After this I stayed in Bristol about a week and then passed with Margaret into the country to Olveston, where Margaret passed homewards towards the north and I passed on in the work of the Lord into Wiltshire, where I had many large and precious meetings.

1670

And whilst I was in the country I heard that Margaret was haled out of her house and carried to Lancaster prison again, an order being gotten from the King and Council to fetch her back into prison again upon her old praemunire, though she was discharged from that imprisonment by an order from the King and his Council the year before.

As soon as I was got to London, I hastened Thomas Lower's wife Mary, and Sarah Fell (two of my wife's daughters) to the King, to acquaint him how their mother was dealt with, and see if they could get a full discharge for her that she might enjoy her estate and liberty without molestation. This was somewhat difficult at first to get, but by diligent attendance on it they at length got an order from the King that their mother should not be molested nor disquieted in the enjoyment of her estate nor house.

After I had been in the country, as I came up the streets in London the drums beat for every household to send forth a soldier into the trained bands, to be in readiness, the Act against seditious conventicles [meetings of more than five persons] being then come into force, and was turned upon us who of all people were free from sedition and tumult. Whereupon I writ the declaration before mentioned, showing from the preamble and terms of the said Act, that we were not such a people, nor our meetings such meetings as were described in that Act.

And as I was going toward Rochester I lighted and walked down a hill: and a great weight and oppression fell on my spirit. So I got on my horse again, but my weight and oppression was so as I was hardly able to ride . . . and very much loaden and burdened with the world's spirits.

But at last I lost my hearing and sight so as I could not see nor hear. And I said unto Friends that I should be as a sign to such as would not see, and such as would not hear the Truth. And in this condition I continued a pretty while. And several people came about me, but I felt their spirits and discerned, though I could not see them, who was honest-hearted and who was not.

And several Friends that were doctors came and would have given me physic but I was not to meddle with their things. And under great sufferings and groans and travails, and sorrows and oppressions, I lay for several weeks.

And one time, when they had given me up, several went away and said they would not see me die; and others said I would be still enough by such a time; and it was all over London and in the country that I was past hopes of recovery and that I was deceased.

And there I lay at the widow Dry's all that winter, warring with the evil spirits, and could not endure the smell of any flesh meat.

And at this time there were great persecutions and there had been searching for me at London, and some meetinghouses plucked down and broken up with soldiers. Sometimes they would come with a troop of horse and a company of foot, and they would break their swords and muskets, carbines and pikes, with beating Friends and wounding abundance, so that the blood stood like puddles in the streets. And Friends were made to stand, by the Lord's power. And some of the formalists would say if Friends did not stand the nation would run into debauchery.

So in my deep misery I saw things beyond words to utter; and I saw a black coffin but I passed over it.

And at last I overcame these spirits and men-eaters though many times I was so weak that people knew not whether I was in the body or out. And many precious Friends came far and nigh to see me and attended upon me and were with me; and towards the spring I began to recover and to walk up and down, to the astonishment of Friends and others.

But they all saw and took notice that as the persecutions ceased I came from under my travails and sufferings.

[Since chapters 23 and 24 of the Journal have been pieced together out of several sources, it is wise simply to summarize their account of George Fox's journey in America, where he traveled in the ministry from 1671 to 1673. Leaving England in August 1671, George Fox and a group of his close companions crossed the Atlantic and spent some seven months in Barbados and Jamaica before they made the crossing to Virginia, arriving there in April 1672. From Virginia, using Indian guides and where possible horses and small boats, they made their way north through bogs and swamps and trackless forests to Boston. They then retraced their course and extended it as far as Carolina before returning to Virginia in order to embark for England. They arrived in Bristol some two months short of two years from the date of their departure.

In the course of this perilous journey, stops were made to visit isolated Friends and to help in the ordering of the small Friends groups that they encountered. In addition to nurturing Friends, Fox was called upon in almost every populated region to speak to large groups of colonists who were of many denominations and of none. In not a few of these there were vigorous public encounters with local religious leaders. Fox did not neglect the Indians and on several occasions met with their kings in moving conversations. Uneasy over the slavery that he found, especially in the Caribbean, he warned the owners of slaves to treat them with generous concern and to free them after thirty years of servitude.

At the close of his return journey to England, the Journal contains what is almost a prayer of thanksgiving that in its outpouring of gratitude does not conceal what the journey had cost him:]

1673

The great Lord God of heaven and earth and creator of all, who is over all, carried us by his high hand and mighty power and wisdom over all, and through many dangers and perils by sea and land; and perils of deceitful professors without possession, who were as the raging waves of the sea, but made a calm; and perils of wolves, bears, tigers, and lions; and perils of rattlesnakes and other venomous creatures of like poisonous nature; and perils through great swamps, and bogs, and the wilderness, where no way was, but for such-like creatures, where we travelled and lodged in the nights by fires; and perils over great bays, creeks, and rivers, in open small boats and small canoes; and perils in great storms and tempests in the ocean, which many times were beyond words to utter; and great perils through the Indian countries in the woods or wildernesses by man-eaters, some whereof lay in wait for some of our company that passed from us, but they were discovered, for the Lord's power gave them dominion over all; and great perils by night through the cold, rain, frosts, snow, in lying in the woods and wilderness several nights together until some of our company had their hands and fingers benumbed, whenas some of the world at such times have had their noses and some their fingers and toes frozen off (I was an eye witness of some of these things); and perils of robbers by land and pirates by sea, these troublesome times, whereof the sea abounds.

The Lord was our convoy; the Lord God steered our course; the Lord God, who rides upon the wings of the wind, ordered our winds for us.

[Notified of his return to Bristol, the reunion with his family and Friends is swiftly described:]

And Margaret (Fell), and Thomas Lower (her son-in-law) with two of her daughters, Sarah Fell and Rachel Fell, came up to Bristol to me out of the North, and John Rous and William Penn and his wife, and Gerald Roberts came down from London to see us; and many Friends from several parts of the nation came to see us at the fair.

Glorious, powerful meetings we had there, and the Lord's infinite power and life was over all. I was moved to declare: God was the first teacher, in Paradise; and whilst man kept under his teaching he was happy. . . . They that come to be renewed up again into

the divine heavenly image, in which man was first made, will
know the same God, that was the first teacher of Adam and Eve in
Paradise, to speak to them now by his son who changes not. Glory
be to his name for ever.

The clearness of persons proposing marriage more closely and
strictly inquired into in the wisdom of God; and all the members
of the spiritual body, the Church, might watch over and be helpful to each other in love.

And after the Women's Meetings were settled in those countries, and I had many precious meetings amongst Friends. . . .

And after I had stayed a while in London I passed with Margaret
and Rachel Fell into the country to Hendon and from thence to
William Penn's at Rickmansworth in Hertfordshire, where Thomas
Lower came to us the next day to accompany us on our journey
northward.

And as I was sitting at supper that night before the morning I
went away, I felt I was taken, yet said nothing to anybody of it
then.

At Armscote in Tredington parish, we had a very large and precious meeting in his barn and the Lord's powerful presence was
amongst us.

And after the meeting was done and Friends many of them gone,
as I was sitting in the parlour with some Friends, discoursing, there

came one Justice Parker and a priest called Rowland Harris, priest of Honington, to the house. Though there was no meeting when they came, yet Henry Parker took me, and Thomas Lower for company with me; and though he had nothing to lay to our charge, sent us both to Worcester gaol by a strange sort of mittimus. . . .

Being thus made prisoners, without any probable appearance of being released before the Quarter Sessions at soonest, we got some Friends to accompany my wife and her daughter into the north, and we were conveyed to Worcester gaol.

1674

[In a letter of George Fox to George Whitehead and others in London:]

> [At the Sessions] the chairman stood up and said, "You Mr. Fox are a famous man and all this may be true that you have said. But, that we may be better satisfied, will you take the Oath of Allegiance and Supremacy?" Then I told them it was a snare; and then they caused the oath to be read. And when they had done I told them, I never took an oath in my life. . . .
>
> And when I was speaking what I could say instead of the oath they cried, "Give him the book." And I said, "The book says, 'Swear not at all'"; and then they cried, "Take him away gaoler, take him away.". . .
>
> Thomas Lower, though he is at liberty, won't leave me, but stays with me in prison till he see

what may be done concerning me. So no more
but my love,

George Fox

After I had been a prisoner at Worcester, soon after the Sessions
were over I was removed to London by a *habeas corpus* for the sher-
iff to bring me up to the King's Bench bar.

[Nine months later: Oct. 1674]

Endeavours were used to get me released, at least for a time, till I
was grown stronger; but the way of effecting it proved difficult
and tedious; for the King was not willing to release me by any
other way than a pardon, being told he could not legally do it;
and I was not willing to be released by a pardon, which he
would readily have given me, because I did not look upon that
way as agreeable with the innocency of my cause.

After this, my wife went to London, and spoke to the King, laying
before him my long and unjust imprisonment, with the manner
of my being taken, and the justices' proceedings against me in
tendering me the oath as a snare, whereby they had praemunired
me; so that I being now his prisoner, it was in his power and at
his pleasure to release, which she desired. The King spoke kindly
to her, and referred her to the lord-keeper, to whom she went,
but could not obtain what she desired; for he said the King could
not release me otherwise than by a pardon; and I was not free to
receive a pardon, knowing I had not done evil.

1675

[In the king's court in London his case was finally brought before Judge Hale, the chief justice.]

I was set at liberty the 12th day of the 12th month 1674 [February 1675] by the Lord Chief Justice Hale, upon a trial of the errors in my indictment, without receiving any pardon or coming under any obligation or engagement at all. And the Lord's everlasting power went over all to his glory and praise, and to the magnifying of his name for ever, Amen. Thus from the 17th of 10th month [December] 1673, was I kept a prisoner and tossed to and from Worcester to London and from London to Worcester again three times, and so kept a prisoner till the 12th of 12th month 1674 [February 1675], being one year and near two months.

And so when I was set at liberty, having been very weak, I passed to Kingston after I had visited Friends in London. And after I had stayed a while there and visited Friends I came to London again. And I writ a paper to the Parliament and sent several books to them. And several papers out of divers parts of the nation were sent up to the King and Parliament from Friends. And a great book against swearing was given to them, which so influenced many of them it was thought they would have done something for our relief therein if they had sat longer.

The Truth sprang up first, to us so as to be a people to the Lord, in Leicestershire in 1644, in Warwickshire in 1645, in

Nottinghamshire in 1646, in Derbyshire in 1647, and in the adja-
cent counties in 1648, 1649, and 1650; and in Yorkshire in 1651,
and in Lancashire and Westmorland in 1652, and in Cumberland,
Bishoprick, and Northumberland in 1653, in London and most
parts of the nation and Scotland and Ireland in 1654. And in 1655
many went beyond seas, where Truth also sprang up. And in 1656
Truth broke forth in America and in many other places.

And the Truth stood all the cruelties and sufferings that were
inflicted upon Friends by the Long Parliament and then by Oliver
Protector, and all the Acts that Oliver Protector made, and his Parliaments, and his son Richard after him, and the Committee of Safety.

And after, it withstood and lasted out all the Acts and Procla-
mations, since 1660 that the King came in. And still the Lord's
Truth is over all and his Seed reigns and his Truth exceedingly
spreads unto this year 1676.

[George Fox died in 1691, some fifteen years after the concluding of his Journal.
In the Nickalls edition of the Journal, these later years in Fox's life are covered by
an able essay written by the late Henry J. Cadbury. Fox spent less than two of these
later years (1678–1680) at Swarthmoor Hall in the north of England. For the
balance of the time, he used London as his base and both counseled and personally
participated in strengthening the structure and especially the spiritual nurture of
the vast cluster of Monthly Meetings that were spread like a net over Britain. His
moving epistles continued to rouse Friends, and his ministry and the prayers that
sprang up in the meetings for worship did not wane in their power to the very end
of his life. In these later years he shared in two visits to the Continent (1677 and
1684), traveling with seasoned Friends and visiting principally the Netherlands and

a few cities in northwestern Germany. The Dutch Yearly Meeting was established in the first of these visits.

George Fox encouraged his fellow Quaker William Penn in his concern to establish a colony in America that was referred to as "A Holy Experiment." In 1681, King Charles II was persuaded to settle a sizable debt that was owed to the estate of Penn's deceased father, Admiral Penn, by granting to William Penn the proprietorship of a vast tract of land in America that was to become known as Pennsylvania. William Penn left England on August 13, 1682, in order to set up his new colony. He was accompanied and followed by thousands of Quakers whom he had invited to leave their homelands in order to colonize the new territory whose constitution promised full religious liberty to all.

As late as 1686 there were still 1,460 Quakers in prison in Britain. This persistent persecution, countered by the unbending refusal of Friends to give up their right to worship in their own way, which Fox and his companions bravely maintained, kept swelling the numbers of British Friends who chose to cross the ocean in order to be free to follow their inward Guide and to raise their families in a climate where their Quaker testimonies were respected.

George Fox lived to see Britain's bloodless revolution of 1688 and a lessening of pressure upon his Quaker movement in the years that followed. A careful study of British history in this period from 1660 to 1689 would be compelled to make more than a footnote of the sizable influence exerted by the unflinching, nonviolent Quaker willingness to suffer for full religious freedom to worship God as they were drawn to do in securing the new freedom for all, which the revision of the laws in 1689 accomplished.

George Fox died in 1691 at the age of sixty-seven. Two of his exclamations at the very close of his life have been preserved: "Now I am clear. I am fully clear." "All is well. The Seed of God reigns over all, and over death itself. And though I am weak in body, yet the power of God is over all, and the Seed reigns over disorderly spirits."]

THE JOURNAL
OF JOHN WOOLMAN

John Woolman (1720–1772)

Over the years, John Woolman's Journal has become an American classic. It would be difficult to find, among the many journals that appeared in the ranks of the Quakers who flourished in colonial America in the eighteenth century, one that could compare with it. It was the favorite of Charles Lamb, who wrote, "Get the writings of John Woolman by Heart." In 1871, the poet Whittier issued a little-changed edition of the Journal, adding a long informative introduction. This Whittier edition went through a number of printings. It was not by accident that Harvard's president, Charles William Eliot, selected Woolman's Journal for the "Five Foot Book Shelf" he edited early in this century. The edition that has been chosen here for abridgment was made by Phillip Moulton and published by the Oxford University Press in 1971. It is generally regarded as the most carefully researched and edited version of the Journal that we possess.

Although the Journal is written with restraint and a strong note of understatement that is not absent from other Quaker journals of that period, it is able to communicate a plain and honest account of a "collected" life. Woolman had his seasons of lower visibility, of getting away from the root, of running ahead of or lagging behind his Inward Guide. Yet he knew his way back, and he used what he knew. The flashes of sanctity that his Journal, with all its modesty, unveil are always enclosed in the earthy humanity of the husband and father, the tailor and orchardman, the respected member of a small colonial New Jersey town and a beloved member of his own Quaker meeting. His frankness about his own human—all too human—hesitations and their overcoming add to the authenticity of the Journal.

Woolman's Journal is not only the story of a "collected" man but is also the recounting of the way in which a Quaker "concern" may unfold within a man's heart and, if attended to and followed out, may not only reshape his own life as its vehicle but also spread to others and become a transforming power in the history of his time. In his concern to right the wrong of holding slaves, Woolman confronted a custom that was as fully accepted among many of the Quakers in his generation as the ownership of stocks and bonds or a bank account that bears interest might be in our own.

As was customary among Friends, Woolman always secured time from his local meeting to travel in the ministry, taking a companion with him when he made his periodic journeys first into Maryland, Virginia, and Carolina, later to New England. He visited meetings and Quaker families, bringing his quiet but often painful message asking for the freeing of any slaves that Quakers might hold and the provision for their future well being.

He began these journeys in 1746. By the time of his early death in 1772, his faithfulness to his concern and the widespread support of those who associated themselves with him had opened the Quakers of colonial America to a new dimension of their responsibility to their black brothers and sisters and had all but cleared Quaker membership of the holding of slaves. In the course of his traveling in the ministry on this spiritually centered social mission, the Journal reveals the outlines of a highly creative, nonviolent approach to the resolution of conflict, an approach that is striking in its contemporary relevance.

—DOUGLAS V. STEERE

Chapter 1

1720–1742

I have often felt a motion of love to leave some hints in writing of my experience of the goodness of God, and now, in the thirty-sixth year of my age, I begin this work. I was born in Northampton, in Burlington County in West Jersey, A.D. 1720, and before I was seven years old I began to be acquainted with the operations of divine love. Through the care of my parents I was taught to read near as soon as I was capable of it, and as I went from school one Seventh-day, I remember, while my companions went to play by the way, I went forward out of sight; and sitting down, I read the twenty-second chapter of the Revelations: "He showed me a river of water, clear as crystal, proceeding out of the throne of God and the Lamb, etc." And in reading it my mind was drawn to seek after that pure habitation which I then believed God had prepared for his servants. The place where I sat and the sweetness that attended my mind remains fresh in my memory.

This and the like gracious visitations had that effect upon me, that when boys used ill language it troubled me, and through the continued mercies of God I was preserved from it.

Another thing remarkable in my childhood was that once, going to a neighbor's house, I saw on the way a robin sitting on her nest; and as I came near she went off, but having young ones, flew about and with many cries expressed her concern for them.

I stood and threw stones at her, till one striking her, she fell down dead. At first I was pleased with the exploit, but after a few minutes was seized with horror, as having in a sportive way killed an innocent creature while she was careful for her young. I beheld her lying dead and thought those young ones for which she was so careful must now perish for want of their dam to nourish them; and after some painful considerations on the subject, I climbed up the tree, took all the young birds and killed them, supposing that better than to leave them to pine away and die miserably, and believed in this case that Scripture proverb was fulfilled, "The tender mercies of the wicked are cruel" [Prov. 12:10]. I then went on my errand, but for some hours could think of little else but the cruelties I had committed, and was much troubled.

Thus he whose tender mercies are over all his works hath placed a principle in the human mind which incites to exercise goodness toward every living creature; and this being singly attended to, people become tender-hearted and sympathizing, but being frequently and totally rejected, the mind shuts itself up in a contrary disposition.

About the twelfth year of my age, my father being abroad, my mother reproved me for some misconduct, to which I made an undutiful reply; and the next First-day as I was with my father returning from meeting, he told me he understood I had behaved amiss to my mother and advised me to be more careful in future. I knew myself blamable, and in shame and confusion remained silent. Being thus awakened to a sense of my wickedness, I felt remorse in my mind, and getting home I retired and prayed to the Lord to forgive me, and do not remember that I ever after that spoke unhandsomely to either of my parents, however foolish in other things.

Having attained the age of sixteen years, I began to love wanton company, and though I was preserved from profane language or scandalous conduct, still I perceived a plant in me which produced much wild grapes. Running in this road I found many like myself, and we associated in that which is reverse to true friendship.

But in this swift race it pleased God to visit me with sickness, so that I doubted of recovering. And then did darkness, horror, and amazement with full force seize me, even when my pain and distress of body was very great. I thought it would have been better for me never to have had a being than to see the day which I now saw. I was filled with confusion, and in great affliction both of mind and body I lay and bewailed myself. I had not confidence to lift up my cries to God, whom I had thus offended, but in a deep sense of my great folly I was humbled before him, and at length that word which is as a fire and a hammer broke and dissolved my rebellious heart. And then my cries were put up in contrition, and in the multitude of his mercies I found inward relief, and felt a close engagement that if he was pleased to restore my health, I might walk humbly before him.

After my recovery this exercise remained with me a considerable time; but by degrees giving way to youthful vanities, they gained strength, and getting with wanton young people I lost ground. The Lord had been very gracious and spoke peace to me in the time of my distress, and I now most ungratefully turned again to folly, on which account at times I felt sharp reproof but did not get low enough to cry for help. I was not so hardy as to commit things scandalous, but to exceed in vanity and promote mirth was my chief study. Still I retained a love and esteem for pious people, and their company brought an awe upon me.

In a while I resolved totally to leave off some of my vanities, but there was a secret reserve in my heart of the more refined part of them, and I was not low enough to find true peace. Thus for some months I had great trouble, there remaining in me an unsubjected will which rendered my labours fruitless, till at length through the merciful continuance of heavenly visitations I was made to bow down in spirit before the Lord.

I kept steady to meetings, spent First-days after noon chiefly in reading the Scriptures and other good books, and was early convinced in my mind that true religion consisted in an inward life, wherein the heart doth love and reverence God the Creator and learn to exercise true justice and goodness, not only towards all men but also towards the brute creatures; that as the mind was moved on an inward principle to love God as an invisible, incomprehensible being, on the same principle it was moved to love him in all his manifestations in the visible world; that as by his breath the flame of life was kindled in all animal and sensitive creatures, to say we love God as unseen and at the same time exercise cruelty towards the least creature moving by his life, or by life derived from him, was a contradiction in itself.

I found no narrowness respecting sects and opinions, but believed that sincere, upright-hearted people in every Society who truly loved God were accepted of him.

As I lived under the Cross and simply followed the openings of Truth, my mind from day to day was more enlightened; my former acquaintance was left to judge of me as they would, for I found it safest for me to live in private and keep these things sealed up in my own breast.

While I silently ponder on that change wrought in me, I find no language equal to it nor any means to convey to another a clear idea of it. I looked upon the works of God in this visible creation and an awfulness covered me; my heart was tender and often contrite, and a universal love to my fellow creatures increased in me. This will be understood by such who have trodden in the same path.

Now though I had been thus strengthened to bear the Cross, I still found myself in great danger, having many weaknesses attending me and strong temptations to wrestle with, in the feeling whereof I frequently withdrew into private places and often with tears besought the Lord to help me, whose gracious ear was open to my cry.

All this time I lived with my parents and wrought on the plantation, and having had schooling pretty well for a planter, I used to improve myself in winter evenings and other leisure times. And being now in the twenty-first year of my age, a man in much business shopkeeping and baking asked me if I would hire with him to tend shop and keep books. I acquainted my father with the proposal, and after some deliberation it was agreed for me to go.

At home I had lived retired, and now having a prospect of being much in the way of company, I felt frequent and fervent cries in my heart to God, the Father of Mercies, that he would preserve me from all taint and corruption, that in this more public employ I might serve him, my gracious Redeemer, in that humility and self-denial with which I had been in a small degree exercised in a very private life.

The man who employed me furnished a shop in Mount Holly, about five miles from my father's house and six from his own, and there I lived alone and tended his shop. Shortly after my settlement here I was visited by several young people, my former acquaintance, who knew not but vanities would be as agreeable to me now as ever; and at these times I cried to the Lord in secret for wisdom and strength, for I felt myself encompassed with difficulties and had fresh occasion to bewail the follies of time past in contracting a familiarity with a libertine people. And as I had now left my father's house outwardly, I found my Heavenly Father to be merciful to me beyond what I can express.

By day I was much amongst people and had many trials to go through, but in evenings I was mostly alone and may with thankfulness acknowledge that in those times the spirit of supplication was often poured upon me, under which I was frequently exercised and felt my strength renewed.

After a while my former acquaintance gave over expecting me as one of their company, and I began to be known to some whose conversation was helpful to me. And now, as I had experienced the love of God through Jesus Christ to redeem me from many pollutions and to be a succour to me through a sea of conflicts, with which no person was fully acquainted, and as my heart was often enlarged in this heavenly principle, I felt a tender compassion for the youth who remained entangled in snares like those which had entangled me. From one month to another this love and tenderness increased, and my mind was more strongly engaged for the good of my fellow creatures.

I went to meetings in an awful frame of mind and endeavoured to be inwardly acquainted with the language of the True Shepherd. And one day being under a strong exercise of spirit, I stood up and said some words in a meeting, but not keeping close to the divine opening, I said more than was required of me; and being soon sensible of my error, I was afflicted in mind some weeks without any light or comfort, even to that degree that I could take satisfaction in nothing. I remembered God and was troubled, and in the depth of my distress he had pity upon me and sent the Comforter. I then felt forgiveness for my offense, and my mind became calm and quiet, being truly thankful to my gracious Redeemer for his mercies. And after this, feeling the spring of divine love opened and a concern to speak, I said a few words in a meeting, in which I found peace. This I believe was about six weeks from the first time, and as I was thus humbled and disciplined under the Cross, my understanding became more strengthened to distinguish the language of the pure Spirit which inwardly moves upon the heart and taught [me] to wait in silence sometimes many weeks together, until I felt that rise which prepares the creature to stand like a trumpet through which the Lord speaks to his flock.

In the management of my outward affairs I may say with thankfulness I found Truth to be my support, and I was respected in my master's family, who came to live in Mount Holly within two years after my going there.

About the twenty-third year of my age, I had many fresh and heavenly openings in respect to the care and providence of the Almighty over his creatures in general, and over man as the most noble amongst those which are visible. And being clearly convinced in my judgment that to place my whole trust in God was best for me, I felt renewed engagements that in all things I might act on an inward principle of virtue and pursue worldly business no further than as Truth opened my way therein.

About the time called Christmas I observed many people from the country and dwellers in town who, resorting to the public houses, spent their time in drinking and vain sports, tending to corrupt one another, on which account I was much troubled. At one house in particular there was much disorder, and I believed it was a duty laid on me to go and speak to the master of that house. I considered I was young and that several elderly Friends in town had opportunity to see these things, and though I would gladly have been excused, yet I could not feel my mind clear.

The exercise was heavy, and as I was reading what the Almighty said to Ezekiel respecting his duty as a watchman, the matter was set

home more clearly; and then with prayer and tears I besought the
Lord for his assistance, who in loving-kindness gave me a resigned
heart. Then at a suitable opportunity I went to the public house, and
seeing the man amongst a company, I went to him and told him I
wanted to speak with him; so we went aside, and there in the fear
and dread of the Almighty I expressed to him what rested on my
mind, which he took kindly, and afterward showed more regard to
me than before. In a few years after, he died middle-aged, and I
often thought that had I neglected my duty in that case it would
have given me great trouble, and I was humbly thankful to my gracious Father, who had supported me herein.

My employer, having a Negro woman, sold her and directed me
to write a bill of sale, the man being waiting who bought her. The
thing was sudden, and though the thoughts of writing an instrument of slavery for one of my fellow creatures felt uneasy, yet I
remembered I was hired by the year, that it was my master who
directed me to do it, and that it was an elderly man, a member of
our Society, who bought her; so through weakness I gave way and
wrote it, but at the executing it, I was so afflicted in my mind that
I said before my master and the Friend that I believed slavekeeping
to be a practice inconsistent with the Christian religion. This in
some degree abated my uneasiness, yet as often as I reflected seriously upon it I thought I should have been clearer if I had desired
to be excused from it as a thing against my conscience, for such it
was. And some time after this a young man of our Society spake to
me to write an instrument of slavery, he having lately taken a
Negro into his house. I told him I was not easy to write it, for

though many kept slaves in our Society, as in others, I still believed the practice was not right, and desired to be excused from writing [it]. I spoke to him in good will, and he told me that keeping slaves was not altogether agreeable to his mind, but that the slave being a gift made to his wife, he had accepted of her.

Chapter 2

1743–1748

Having now been several years with my employer, and he doing less at merchandise than heretofore, I was thoughtful of some other way of business, perceiving merchandise to be attended with much cumber in the way of trading in these parts. My mind through the power of Truth was in a good degree weaned from the desire of outward greatness, and I was learning to be content with real conveniences that were not costly, so that a way of life free from much entanglements appeared best for me, though the income was small. I had several offers of business that appeared profitable, but did not see my way clear to accept of them, as believing the business proposed would be attended with more outward care and cumber than was required of me to engage in. I saw that a humble man with the blessing of the Lord might live on a little, and that where the heart was set on greatness, success in business did not satisfy the craving, but that in common with an increase of wealth the desire of wealth increased. There was a care on my mind to so pass my time as to things outward that nothing might hinder me from the most steady attention to the voice of the True Shepherd.

My employer, though now a retailer of goods, was by trade a tailor and kept a servant man at that business; and I began to think about learning the trade, expecting that if I should settle, I might by this trade and a little retailing of goods get a living in a plain way without the load of great business. I mentioned it to my employer and we soon agreed on terms, and then when I had leisure from the affairs of merchandise, I worked with his man. I believed the hand of Providence pointed out this business for me and was taught to be content with it, though I felt at times a disposition that would have sought for something greater. But through the revelation of Jesus Christ, I had seen the happiness of humility, and there was an earnest desire in me to enter deep into it; and at times this desire arose to a degree of fervent supplication, wherein my soul was so environed with heavenly light and consolation that things were made easy to me which had been otherwise.

In the year [blank] my employer's wife died. She was a virtuous woman and generally beloved of her neighbours; and soon after this he left shopkeeping and we parted. I then wrought at my trade as a tailor, carefully attended meetings for worship and discipline, and found an enlargement of gospel love in my mind and therein a concern to visit Friends in some of the back settlements of Pennsylvania and Virginia. And being thoughtful about a companion, I expressed it to my beloved friend Isaac Andrews, who then told me that he had drawings there and also to go through Maryland, Virginia, and Carolina. After considerable time passed and several conferences with him, I felt easy to accompany him throughout, if way opened for it. I opened the case in our Monthly Meeting, and Friends expressing their unity therewith, we obtained certificates to travel as companions—his from Haddonfield and mine from Burlington.

So we took the meetings in our way through Virginia, were in some degree baptized into a feeling sense of the conditions of the people, and our exercise in general was more painful in these old settlements than it had been amongst the back inhabitants. But through the goodness of our Heavenly Father, the well of living waters was at times opened, to our encouragement and the refreshment of the sincere-hearted.

We went on to Perquimans River in North Carolina, had several meetings which were large, and found some openness in those parts and a hopeful appearance amongst the young people. So we turned again to Virginia.

Two things were remarkable to me in this journey. First in regard to my entertainment: When I ate, drank, and lodged free-cost with people who lived in ease on the hard labour of their slaves, I felt uneasy; and as my mind was inward to the Lord, I found, from place to place, this uneasiness return upon me at times through the whole visit. Where the masters bore a good share of the burden and lived frugal, so that their servants were well provided for and their labour moderate, I felt more easy; but where they lived in a costly way and laid heavy burdens on their slaves, my exercise was often great, and I frequently had conversation with them in private concerning it. Secondly, this trade of importing them from their native country being much encouraged amongst them and the white people and their children so generally living without much labour was frequently the subject of my serious thoughts. And I saw in these southern provinces so many vices and corruptions increased by this trade and this way of life that it appeared to me as a dark gloominess hanging over the land; and though now many willingly run into it, yet in future the consequence will be grievous to posterity! I express it as it hath appeared to me, not at once nor twice, but as a matter fixed on my mind.

The winter following died my eldest sister, Elizabeth Woolman, Jr., of the smallpox, aged 31 years. She was from her youth of a thoughtful disposition and very compassionate to her acquaintance in their sickness or distress, being ready to help as far as she could.

Of late I found drawings in my mind to visit Friends in New England, and having an opportunity of joining in company with my beloved friend Peter Andrews, we, having obtained certificates from our Monthly Meeting, set forward 16th day, 3rd month, 1747, and reached the Yearly Meeting on Long Island.

In this journey I may say in general we were sometimes in much weakness and laboured under discouragements, and at other times, through the renewed manifestations of divine love, we had reasons of refreshment wherein the power of Truth prevailed.

We were taught by renewed experience to labour for an inward stillness, at no time to seek for words, but to live in the spirit of Truth and utter that to the people which Truth opened in us. My beloved companion and I belonged both to one meeting, came forth in the ministry near together, and were inwardly united in the work. He was about thirteen years older than I, bore the heaviest burden, and was an instrument of the greatest use.

Chapter 9

1763–1769

Notes at our Yearly Meeting at Philadelphia, 9th month, 1764. First John Smith of Marlborough, aged upward of eighty years, a faithful minister though not eloquent, in our meeting of ministers and elders on the 25th stood up and, appearing to be under a great exercise of spirit, informed Friends in substance as follows, to wit: that he had been a member of the Society upward of sixty years and well remembered that in those early times Friends were a plain, lowly-minded people, and that there was much tenderness and contrition in their meetings; that at the end of twenty years from that time, the Society increasing in wealth and in some degree conforming to the fashions of the world, true humility was less apparent and their meetings in general not so lively and edifying; that at the end of forty years many of them were grown very rich—that wearing of fine costly

garments and using of silver (and other) watches became customary with them, their sons, and their daughters, and many of
the Society made a specious appearance in the world, which
marks of outward wealth and greatness appeared on many in our
meetings of ministers and elders, and as these things became
more prevalent, so the powerful overshadowings of the Holy
Ghost were less manifest in the Society, that there had been a
continued increase of these ways of life even until now, and that
the weakness which hath now overspread the Society and the
barrenness manifest amongst us is matter of much sorrow.

He then mentioned the uncertainty of his attending these
meetings in future, expecting his dissolution was now near, and
signified that he had seen in the true light that the Lord would
bring back his people from these things into which they were
thus degenerated but that his faithful servants must first go
through great and heavy exercises therein.

29th day, 9th month, 1764. The committee appointed by the
Yearly Meeting some time since now made report in writing of their
proceedings in that service, in which they signified that in the course
of their proceedings they had been apprehensive that some persons
holding offices in government inconsistent with our principles and
others who kept slaves—these remaining active members in our
meetings of discipline—had been one means of weakness more and
more prevailing in the management thereof in some places.

After this report was read, an exercise revived on my mind
which at times had attended me several years, and inward cries to
the Lord were raised in me that the fear of man might not prevent

me from doing what he required of me; and standing up I spake in substance as follows:

I've felt a tenderness in my mind toward persons in two circumstances mentioned in that report—that is, toward such active members who keep slaves and such who hold offices in civil government—and have desired that Friends in all their conduct may be kindly affectioned one toward another. Many Friends who keep slaves are under some exercise on that account and at times think about trying them with freedom, but find many things in their way. And the way of living and annual expenses of some of them are such that it is impracticable for them to set their slaves free without changing their own way of life. It has been my lot to be often abroad, and I have observed in some places, at Quarterly and Yearly Meetings and at some stages where travelling Friends and their horses are often entertained, that the yearly expense of individuals therein is very considerable. And Friends in some places crowding much on persons in these circumstances for entertainment hath often rested as a burden on my mind for some years past, and I now express it in the fear of the Lord, greatly desiring that Friends now present may duly consider it.

In fifty pounds are four hundred half crowns. If a slave be valued at fifty pounds and I with my horse put his owner to half a crown expense, and I with many others for a course of years repeat these expense [sic] four hundred times, then on a fair computation this slave may be accounted a slave to the public under the direction of the man he calls master.

QUAKER STRONGHOLDS
BY CAROLINE STEPHEN

Caroline Stephen (1834–1909)

Precisely a century after John Woolman's death at York (1772), Caroline Stephen was taken to her first Friends Meeting for Worship, where she at last discovered herself to be spiritually at home. She belonged to a most distinguished British family. Her father, Sir James Stephen, had been Regius Professor of History at Cambridge. Her brother, Sir Leslie Stephen, was a brilliant writer of his time, and his daughter, Caroline's niece, was Virginia Woolf.

Caroline Stephen became a Friend by convincement and blessed the Quakers with a highly articulate account of what she had personally found to be authentic in their witness. Her Quaker Strongholds, which appeared in 1890 and has gone through several printings, is a Quaker classic, and the selections that are made here are all, with one exception, taken from it. Two years after her death, Thomas Hodgkin wrote a brief memoir, Caroline Stephen and the Society of Friends. An introductory paragraph summing up her Quaker insights is so telling that I have included it in this foreword:

> The fundamental truth which underlay all the teaching of George Fox and the Early Friends was this: God, who spoke of old to His people by the mouth of prophets and apostles, and who gave the fullest revelation of Himself in the person of Jesus Christ, still speaks; and we may every one of us, if we will, hear that Divine Voice in the secret of our hearts. "Both before and since His blessed manifestation in the flesh, Christ has been the light and life, the rock and strength, of all that ever feared God; present with them in their temptations, He follows them in their travels and afflictions, supports and carries them through and over the difficulties that have attended them in their earthly pilgrimage." Or, as George Fox says of one of his meetings, "My message unto them from the Lord was, that they should all come together again and wait to feel the Lord's power and spirit in themselves, to gather them together to Christ, that they

might be taught of Him who says, 'Learn of Me.'" This is, of course, Mysticism, but it is also the setting forth of a truth not formally denied by any section of the Christian Church, though few have felt it so intensely or preached it so persistently as the Early Friends. In their advocacy of this doctrine, and in their obedience to what they conceived to be its practical consequences, they suffered bitter persecution both from Roundhead and Cavalier, did many noble deeds, and spoke some unwise and unmeasured words, but displayed a new and much needed type of Christianity to the world.

—DOUGLAS V. STEERE

Quaker Strongholds

The notorious disinclination of Friends to any attempts at prose-lytizing, and perhaps some lingering effects of persecution, probably account for the very common impression that Friends' meetings are essentially private—mysterious gatherings into which it would be intrusive to seek admission.

Some such vague impression floated, I believe, over my own mind, when, some seventeen years ago, I first found myself within reach of a Friends' meeting, and, somewhat to my surprise, cordially made welcome to attend it. The invitation came at a moment of need, for I was beginning to feel with dismay that I might not much longer be able conscientiously to continue to join in the Church of England service.

At any rate, it was fast leading me to dread the moment when I should be unable either to find the help I needed, or to offer my tribute of devotion in any place of worship amongst my fellow Christians. When lo, on one never-to-be-forgotten Sunday morning, I found myself one of a small company of silent worshipers, who were content to sit down together without words, that each one might feel after and draw near to the divine Presence, unhindered at least, if not helped, by any human utterance. Utterance I knew was free, should the words be given; and before the meeting was over, a sentence or two were uttered in great simplicity by an old and apparently untaught man, rising in this place amongst the rest of us. I did not pay much attention to the words he spoke, and I have no recollection of their purport. My whole soul was filled with the unutterable peace of the undisturbed opportunity for communion with God, with the sense that at last I had found a place where I might, without the faintest suspicion of insincerity, join with others in simply seeking his presence. To sit down in silence could at the least pledge me to nothing; it might open to me (as it did that morning) the very gate of heaven. And since that day, now more than seventeen years ago, Friends' meetings have indeed been to me the greatest of outward helps to a fuller and fuller entrance into the spirit from which they have sprung; the place of the most soul-subduing, faith-restoring, strengthening, and peaceful communion, in feeding upon the bread of life, that I have ever known. I cannot but believe that what has helped me so unspeakably might be helpful to multitudes in this day of shaking of all that can be shaken, and of restless inquiry after spiritual good. It is in the hope of making more widely known the true source and nature of such spiritual help that I am about to attempt to describe what I have called our strongholds—those principles which cannot fail, whatever may be the future of the Society which for more than two hundred years has taken its stand upon them. I wish to trace, as far as my experience as a "convinced Friend" enables me to do so, what is the true life and strength of our Society; and the manner in which its principles, as actually embodied in its practice, its organization, and, above all, its manner of worship, are fitted to meet the special needs of an important class in our own day.

Organization: Every congregation meeting habitually for worship on the first day of the week is one of a group of probably four or five Monthly Meetings, which in like manner unite to form a Quarterly Meeting, at whose quarterly sittings matters of larger importance are considered, and the eighteen Quarterly Meetings of Great Britain form in their turn the London Yearly Meeting. It may in a certain sense be said, indeed, that it is the Society of Friends of Great Britain, for every Friend is a member of the Monthly, Quarterly, and Yearly Meetings to which he or she belongs, and is entitled to a voice in all their deliberations.

Certain "queries" have from the earliest times been appointed by the authority of the Yearly Meeting, to be read and considered at certain seasons in the subordinate meetings. . . .

The business of the elders is to watch over the [recorded] ministers in the exercise of their gift; that of the overseers to see to the relief of the poorer members, the care of the sick, and other such matters; to watch over the members generally with regard to their Christian conduct, to warn privately any who may be giving cause of offence or scandal, and in case of need to bring the matter before the Monthly Meeting, to be dealt with as it may require.

The very copious biographical literature of the Society teems with the records of journeys undertaken "under an impression of religious duty," and lasting sometimes for months, or even years, before the Friend could "feel clear" of the work. No limit is ever set beforehand to such work. It is felt to be work in which the daily unfolding of the divine ordering must be watched and waited for.

I have already referred to the peculiarity which lies at the root of all the rest; namely, our views as to the nature of the true Gospel ministry, as a call bestowed on men and women, on old and young, learned and unlearned; bestowed directly from above, and not to be conferred by any human authority, or hired for money; to be exercised under the sole and immediate direction of the one Master, the only Head of the Church, Christ the Lord. As a consequence of this view, Friends have, as is well known, refused as a matter of conscience to pay tithes, or in any way to contribute to the maintenance of a paid ministry, and of the services prescribed by the Established Church.

Closely connected with these views on ministry is our testimony against the observance of any religious rites or ceremonies whatever. Neither baptizing with water, nor the breaking of bread and drinking of wine, are recognized by us as divinely ordained institutions of permanent obligation, and neither of these ceremonies is practised by us.

The one corner-stone of belief upon which the Society of Friends is built is the conviction that God does indeed communicate with each one of the spirits he has made, in a direct and living inbreathing of some measure of the breath of his own life; that he never leaves himself without a witness in the heart as well as in the surroundings of man; and that in order clearly to hear the divine voice thus speaking to us we need to be still; to be alone with him in the secret place of his presence; that all flesh should keep silence before him.

The history of the sudden gathering of the Society, of its rapid formation into a strongly organized body, and of the extraordinary constancy, zeal, and integrity displayed by its original members, is a most impressive proof of the trueness of their aim.

When questioned as to the reality and nature of the inner light, the early Friends were accustomed in return to ask the questions whether they did not sometimes feel something within them that showed them their sins; and to assure them that this same power, which *made manifest*, and therefore was truly light, would also, if yielded to, lead them out of sin. This assurance, that the light which revealed was also the power which would heal sin, was George Fox's gospel. The power itself was described by him in many ways. Christ within, the hope of glory; the light, life, Spirit, and grace of Christ; the Seed, the new birth, the power of God unto salvation, and many other such expressions, flow forth in abundant streams to heartfelt eloquence. To "turn people to the light within," to "direct them to Christ, their free Teacher," was his daily business.

The perennial justification of Quakerism lies in its energetic assertion that the kingdom of heaven is within us; that we are not made dependent upon any outward organization for our spiritual welfare. Its perennial difficulty lies in the inveterate disposition of human beings to look to each other for spiritual help, in the feebleness of their perception of that divine voice which speaks to each one in a language no other ear can hear, and in the apathy which is content to go through life without the attempt at any true individual communion with God.

I believe the doctrine of Fox and Barclay (i.e., briefly, that the "Word of God" is Christ, not the Bible, and that the Scriptures are profitable in proportion as they are read in the same spirit which gave them forth) to have been a most valuable equipoise to the tendency of other Protestant sects to transfer the idea of infallibility from the Church to the Bible. Nothing, I believe, can really teach us the nature and meaning of inspiration but personal experience of it. That we may all have such experience if we will but attend to the divine influences in our own hearts, is the cardinal doctrine of Quakerism. Whether this belief, honestly acted on, will manifest itself in the homespun and solid, but only too sober morality of the typical everyday Quaker, or whether it will land us in the mystical fervours of an Isaac Penington, or the apostolic labours of a John Woolman or a Stephen Grellet, must depend chiefly upon our natural temperament and special gifts.

Here we are confronted with the real "peculiarity" of Quakerism—its relation to mysticism. There is no doubt that George Fox himself and the other fathers of the Society were of a strongly mystical turn of mind, though not in the sense in which the word is often used by the worshipers of "common sense," as a mild term of reproach, to convey a general vague dreaminess. Nothing, certainly, could be less applicable to the early Friends that any such reproach as this. They were fiery, dogmatic, pugnacious, and intensely practical and soberminded. But they were assuredly mystics in what I take to be the more accurate sense of that word—people, that is, with a vivid consciousness of the inwardness of the light of truth.

A true mystic believes that all men have, as he himself is conscious of having, an inward life, into which as into a secret chamber, he can retreat at will. In this inner chamber he finds a refuge from the ever-changing aspects of outward existence; from the multitude of cares and pleasures and agitations which belong to the life of the senses and the affections; from human judgments; from all change, and chance, and turmoil, and distraction. He finds there, first repose, then an awful guidance; a light which burns and purifies; a voice which subdues; he finds himself in the presence of his God.

Believing in God, and worshiping him with one's whole heart, trusting him absolutely and loving him supremely, seem to me to be but various stages in the growth of one Seed.

That individual and immediate guidance, in which we recognize that "the finger of God is come unto us," seems to come in, as it were, to complete and perfect the work rough-hewn by morality and conscience. We may liken the laws of our country to the cliffs of our island, over which we rarely feel ourselves in any danger of falling; the moral standard of our social circle to the beaten highway road which we can hardly miss. Our own conscience would then be represented by a fence, by which some parts of the country are enclosed for each one, the road itself at times barred or narrowed. And that divine guidance of which I am speaking could be typified only by the pressure of a hand upon ours, leading us gently to step to the right or the left, to pause or to go forward, in a manner intended for and understood by ourselves alone.

The divine guidance is away from self-indulgence, often away from outward success; through humiliation and failure, and many snares and temptations; over rough roads and against opposing forces—always uphill. Its evidence of success is in the inmost, deepest, most spiritual part of our existence.

It seems to me that nothing but silence can heal the wounds made by disputations in the region of the unseen. No external help, at any rate, has ever in my own experience proved so penetratingly efficacious as the habit of joining in a public worship based upon silence. Its primary attraction for me was in the fact that it pledged me to nothing, and left me altogether undisturbed to seek for help in my own way. But before long I began to be aware that the united and prolonged silences had a far more direct and powerful effect than this. They soon began to exercise a strangely subduing and softening effect upon my mind. There used, after a while, to come upon me a deep sense of awe, as we sat together and waited—for what? In my heart of hearts I knew in whose name we were met together, and who was truly in the midst of us. Never before had his influence revealed itself to me with so much power as in those quiet assemblies.

And another result of the practice of silent waiting for the unseen presence proved to be a singularly effectual preparation of mind for the willing reception of any words which might be offered "in the name of a disciple." The words spoken were indeed often feeble, and always inadequate (as all words must be in relation to divine things), sometimes even entirely irrelevant to my own individual needs, though at other times profoundly impressive and helpful; but, coming as they did after the long silences which had fallen like dew upon the thirsty soil, they went far deeper, and were received into a much less thorny region than had ever been the case with the words I had listened to from the pulpit.

In Friends' meetings also, from the fact that every one is free to speak, one hears harmonies and correspondences between very various utterances such as are scarcely to be met with elsewhere. It is sometimes as part-singing compared with unison.

The free admission of the ministry of women, of course, greatly enriches this harmony. I have often wondered whether some of the motherly counsels I have listened to in our meeting would not reach some hearts that might be closed to the masculine preacher.

But it is not only the momentary effect of silence as a help in public worship that constitutes its importance in Quaker estimation. The silence we value is not the mere outward silence of the lips. It is a deep quietness of heart and mind, a laying aside of all preoccupation with passing things—yes, even with the workings of our own minds; a resolute fixing of the heart upon that which is unchangeable and eternal. This "silence of all flesh" appears to us to be the essential preparation for any act of true worship. It is also, we believe, the essential condition at all times of inward illumination. "Stand still in the light," says George Fox again and again, and then strength comes—and peace and victory and deliverance, and all other good things. "Be still, and know that I am God." It is the experience, I believe, of all those who have been most deeply conscious of his revelations of himself, that they are made emphatically to the "waiting" soul—to the spirit which is most fully conscious of its own inability to do more than wait in silence before him.

THE WRITINGS OF
RUFUS M. JONES

Rufus M. Jones (1863–1948)

It is hard to see how there could be any serious disagreement that in the first half of the twentieth century the weightiest voice that interpreted Quakerism both in its history and in outlining its present and future course was that of Rufus M. Jones. The monumental task of editing and helping to write the six-volume history of the Religious Society of Friends; the large share that he had in founding and guiding the American Friends Service Committee; the quality of his own spiritual life; the stream of books and articles that came from his pen; the power of his ministry and his public service as an interpreter of the spiritual life in that generation, all undergird this assessment of the impact of his life and service. In addition, he taught philosophy at Haverford College for forty years and has left his stamp upon the college and its graduates.

The passages from his writings that have been selected here have been taken from Finding the Trail of Life and The Luminous Trail.

—DOUGLAS V. STEERE

Finding the Trail of Life

I am convinced by my own life and by wide observation of children that mystical experience is much more common than is usually supposed. Children are not so absorbed as we are with things and with problems. They are not so completely organized for dealing with the outside world as we older persons are. They do not live by cut-and-dried theories. They have more room for surprise and wonder. They are more sensitive to intimations, flashes, openings. The invisible impinges on their souls and they feel its reality as something quite natural. Wordsworth was no doubt a rare and unusual child, but many a boy, who was never to be a poet, has felt as he did. "I was often unable," he says, in the preface to his great "Ode," "to think of external things as having external existence, and I communed with all that I saw as something not apart from, but inherent in, my own immaterial nature. Many times while going to school have I grasped at a wall or tree to recall myself from this abyss of idealism to the reality." The world within is just as real as the world without until events force us to become mainly occupied with the outside one.

My roots for many generations were deep in Quaker subsoil. There were, however, some features connected with my arrival which might naturally discourage a newcomer. The house to which I came was most plainly furnished. It was many miles from any city; a cold, bleak winter was at its height—January 25th, 1863—and there seemed to be almost no conveniences for comfort and few preparations for what we usually call culture. But these matters troubled me not a bit. It never occurred to me that this was a world of inequalities and I had no prevision of the struggle by which one wins what he gets.

The only real fact I can relate about these first hours is one which shows what the highest ambition of my family was and it will also illustrate a characteristic trait in the member of my family who did very much to shape my life in those years when I was plastic to the touch. As soon as I came into the arms of my Aunt Peace, my father's oldest sister who lived with us—one of God's saints—she had an "opening" such as often came to her, for she was gifted with prophetic vision, "This child," she said, "will one day bear the message of the Gospel to distant lands and to peoples across the sea." It was spoken solemnly and with a calm assurance as though she saw the little thing suddenly rising out of her lap to go. That prophecy may seem like a simple word but it expressed the highest ideal of that devoted woman, and her faith in the fulfillment never slackened, even when the growing boy showed signs of doing anything else rather than realizing that hope. If the neighbors, in the period of my youth, had been told of this prophecy it would, I am afraid, almost have shaken their faith in the forevision of this remarkable woman whom they all loved and whose insight they implicitly trusted.

While I was too young to have any religion of my own, I had come to a home where religion kept its fires always burning. We had very few "things," but we were rich in invisible wealth. I was not "christened" in a church, but I was sprinkled from morning till night with the dew of religion. We never ate a meal which did not begin with a hush of thanksgiving; we never began a day without "a family gathering" at which mother read a chapter of the Bible, after which there would follow a weighty silence. These silences, during which all the children of our family were hushed with a kind of awe, were very important features of my spiritual development. There was work inside and outside the house waiting to be done, and yet we sat there hushed and quiet, doing nothing. I very quickly discovered that something *real* was taking place. We were feeling our way down to that place from which living words come and very often they did come. Some one would bow and talk with God so simply and quietly that he never seemed far away. The words helped to explain the silence. We were now finding what we had been searching for. When I first began to think of God I did not think of him as very far off. At meeting some of the Friends who prayed shouted loud and strong when they called upon him, but at home he always heard easily and he seemed to be there with us in the living silence. My first steps in religion were thus *acted*. It was a religion which we *did* together. Almost nothing was *said* in the way of instructing me. We all joined together to listen for God and then one of us talked to him for the others. In these simple ways my religious disposition was being unconsciously formed and the roots of my faith in unseen realities were reaching down far below my crude and childish surface thinking.

One of the earliest home memories out of the dim period of "first years" is the return of my Aunt Peace—the aunt of the prophecy—from an extensive religious visit through the Quaker meetings of Ohio and Iowa. I was, of course, most impressed with the things she brought me. They were as wonderful to me as the dark-skinned natives, which Columbus carried back, were to the people who crowded about his returning ship. Iowa was farther off then than the Philippines are now. But the next impression was made by the marvelous stories of special providences and strange leadings which had been experienced on the journey. I listened as though one of the Argonauts was telling of his adventures in search of the Golden Fleece. Every place where there was a Quaker meetinghouse had its peculiar episode which I had told over and over to me. Every little boy whom she had seen and talked with in that far-flung world was described to me and called by name. This was the first event which made me realize that the world was so big. Before this, it seemed to me that it came to an end where the sky touched the hills. But now my aunt had been out beyond the place where the sky came down, and she had found the earth still going on out there! But after all, the most wonderful thing was the way in which God took care of her and told her what to do and to say in every place where she went. It seemed exactly like the things they read to me out of the life of Joseph and Samuel and David, and I supposed that everybody who was good had their lives cared for and guided in this wonderful way. I made up my mind to be good and to be one of the guided kind!

The thing which had the most to do, however, with my deliverance from fear was my childlike discovery that God was with me and that I *belonged to him*. I say "discovery," but it was a discovery slowly made and in the main gathered from the atmosphere of our home. God, as I have said, was as *real* to everybody in our family as was our house or our farm. I soon realized that Aunt Peace *knew* him and that grandmother had lived more than eighty years in intimate relation with him. I caught their simple faith and soon had one of my own. I gradually came to feel assured that whatever might be there in the dark of my bedroom, God anyhow was certainly there, stronger than everything else combined. I learned to whisper to him as soon as I got into bed—I never learned to pray kneeling by the bedside. I never saw anybody do that until I went away to boarding school. I "committed" everything to him. I told him that I couldn't take care of myself and asked him to guard and keep the little boy who needed him. And then, I believed that he would do it. I knew that Aunt Peace never doubted and I tried to follow her plan of life. There were times in my childhood when the God I loved was more real than the things I feared and I am convinced that all children would be genuinely religious if they had someone to lead them rightly to God, to whom they belong.

Everybody at home, as well as many of our visitors, believed implicitly in immediate divine guidance. Those who went out from our meeting to do extended religious service—and there were many such visits undertaken—always seemed as directly selected for these momentous missions as were the prophets of an earlier time. As far back as I can remember, I can see Friends sitting talking with my grandmother of some "concern" which was heavy upon them, and the whole matter seemed as important as though they had been called by an earthly king to carry on the affairs of an empire. It was partly these cases of divine selection and the constant impression that God was using these persons whom I knew to be his messengers that made me so sure of the fact that we were his chosen people. At any rate I grew up with this idea firmly fixed, and the events which will be told in a later chapter deepened the feeling.

When I was ten came one of the crises of my life. It was a great misfortune, which turned out to be a blessing, as is usually the case, if one has eyes to see it. It was the injury to my foot which nearly cost me my leg and seriously threatened my life. Through all the pain and suffering I discovered what a mother's love was.

For nine months I never took a step, and for the first week of my suffering, mother sat by me every night, and I felt her love sweep over me. As soon as I was through the racking pain, something had to be done to entertain me—to make the long hours pass, for everybody in our household was occupied with their own tasks. Grandmother, who was eighty-eight years old, had plenty of leisure, and so it was arranged for us to entertain each other. I decided to read the Bible through out loud to her. She could knit mechanically with flying needles, giving no more attention to her fingers than she did to the movement of the hands on the clock.

Before I began the New Testament I was well enough to go out, so that my reading stopped, and it was not until much later that I got deeply hold of that message which came from the Master. The Old Testament was the book of my boyhood. My heroes and heroines were there. It gave me my first poetry and my first history, and I got my growing ideas of God from it. The idea of choice, the fact that God chose a people and that he chose individuals for his missions, was rooted in my thought.

But greatly as I loved the Bible and devoutly as I believed in my first years that it was to be taken in literal fashion, I am thankful to say that I very early caught the faith and insight, which George Fox and other Quaker leaders had taught, that God is always revealing himself, and that truth is not something finished, but something unfolding as life goes forward. In spite of the fact that I lived in a backwoods community into which modern ideas had not penetrated and belonged to an intensely evangelical family, I nevertheless grew up with an attitude of breadth toward Scripture. I searched it, I loved it, I believed it, but I did not think that God stopped speaking to the human race when "the beloved disciple" finished his last book in the New Testament. The very fact that the spirit of God could impress his thought and will upon holy men of old and had done it made me feel confident that he could continue to do that, and consequently that more light and truth could break through men in our times and in those to come. I cannot be too thankful that that little group of believers who made the Bible my living book and who helped me to find and to love its treasures also had spiritual depth enough to give me the key to a larger freedom that enabled me in later years to keep the Bible still as my book, without at the same time preventing me from making use of all that science and history have revealed or can reveal of God's creative work and of his dealing with men.

Among the many influences which went to form and determine my early life—and so in a measure my whole life—I should give a large place to the visits of itinerant Friends who came to us from far and near. It was a novel custom, this constant interchange of gifted ministers. Something like it apparently prevailed in the early Church, as *The Teaching of the Apostles* indicates, and some of the small religious sects at various periods have maintained an extensive intervisitation, but Friends in the first half of the nineteenth century had developed a form of itinerant ministry which was almost without parallel. It was an admirable method, especially for our rural neighborhoods. We were isolated, and without this contact with the great world we should have had a narrow ingrowing life, but through this splendid spiritual cross-fertilization, we had a chance to increase and improve the quality of our life and thought. The ends of the earth came to our humble door. We got into living contact with Quaker faith and thought in every land where "our religious Society," as we called it, had members. These visitors brought us fresh messages, but, what was not less important, they were themselves unique personalities and were full of incidents and traveler's lore, and thus they formed an excellent substitute for the books which we lacked. They spoke with a prestige and influence which home people seldom have and they brought a contribution into my life which I can hardly overestimate.

Our little local group also had its outgoing stream of itinerant ministry and I was almost as much interested in hearing the story of experiences related by our returning members as I was in listening to the strangers who came among us from afar. My great-uncle drove in his carriage at least twice from Maine to Ohio and Indiana on religious visits, visiting families and attending meetings as he went and living much of the time on his journey in his own carriage. My Aunt Peace made many journeys to remote regions in America and brought back vast stores of information and wisdom. Uncle Eli and Aunt Sybil, who in my youth were among the foremost living Quakers in gift and power of ministry, went back and forth like spiritual shuttles, now weaving their strands of truth into our lives and now again weaving in some far away spot of the earth. It was a very common and ordinary matter for New England Friends to drive to "the Provinces," especially to Nova Scotia, on religious visits, and, as soon as the railroads made travel easy and rapid, there was an almost unbroken stream of circulating ministry.

I felt a certain awe because they always came with "a concern," which means that they had left their homes and had undertaken the long journey because they had received an unmistakable and irresistible call to go out and preach what was given them. This was no ordinary visit. Here was a man under our roof who had come because God sent him. I supposed that he had something inside which had told him to go and where to go.

These itinerant ministers told us of life and work in far-off lands. They interested us with their narratives, and in our narrow life they performed somewhat the service of the wandering minstrel in the days of the old castles. They gave us new experiences, a touch of wider life and farther-reaching associations, and for me, at least, they made the connection with God more real. I got from them a clearer sense of what I might be.

Very often in these meetings for worship, which held usually for nearly two hours, there were long periods of silence, for we never had singing to fill the gaps. I do not think anybody ever told me what the silence was for. It does not seem necessary to explain Quaker silence to children. They feel what it means. They do not know how to use very long periods of hush, but there is something in short, living, throbbing times of silence which finds the child's submerged life and stirs it to nobler living and holier aspiration. I doubt if there is any method of worship which works with a subtler power or which brings into operation in the interior life a more effective moral and spiritual culture. Sometimes a real spiritual wave would sweep over the meeting in these silent hushes, which made me feel very solemn and which carried me—careless boy though I was—down into something which was deeper than my own thoughts, and gave me a momentary sense of that Spirit who has been the life and

light of men in all ages and in all lands. Nobody in this group
had ever heard the word "mystical," and no one would have
known what it meant if it had been applied to this form of worship, but in the best sense of the word this was a mystical religion, and all unconsciously I was being prepared to appreciate
and at a later time to interpret the experience and the life of the
mystics.

In our business meetings, by the world's method, all our business could have been transacted in twenty minutes. We often
spent two hours at it, because every affair had to be soaked in a
spiritual atmosphere until the dew of religion settled on it!
Above in the "high seats" sat two men at a table fastened by
hinges to the minister's rail. This table was swung up and held by
a perpendicular stick beneath. On it lay the old record-book, a
copy of the "discipline," and papers of all sorts. The "clerk," the
main man of the two at the desk, was another of those marvelous beings who seemed to me to know everything by means
of something unseen working inside him! How could he tell
what "Friends" wanted done?—and yet he always knew. No
votes were cast. Everybody said something in his own peculiar
way. A moment of silence would come, and the clerk would rise
and say, "It appears that it is the sense of the meeting" to do thus
and so. Spontaneously from all parts of the house would come
from variously-pitched voices—"I unite with that," "So do I,"
"That is my mind," "I should be easy to have it so." And so we
passed to the next subject.

There were two transactions which were always exciting, and I used each time to live in hope that they would come off. One was "the declaration of intentions of marriage." When such an event occurred the man and woman came in and sat down together, facing the meeting in the completest possible hush. It was an ordeal which made the couple hesitate to rush into marriage until they felt pretty sure that the match was made in heaven. Solemnly they rose, and informed us that they purposed taking each other in marriage, and the parents announced their consent. The meeting "united" and permission was given "to proceed." The marriage itself came off at an even more solemn meeting, when the man and woman took each other "until death should separate." I remember one of these occasions, when the frightened groom took the bride "to be his husband," which made the meeting less solemn than usual.

The other interesting event was the liberation of ministers for religious service "in other parts." If the minister were a woman Friend, as often happened in our meeting, she came in with "a companion." They walked up the aisle and sat down with bowed heads. Slowly the bonnet strings were untied, the bonnet handed to the companion, and the ministering woman rose to say that for a long time the Lord had been calling her to a service in a distant Yearly Meeting; that she had put it off, not feeling that she could undertake so important a work, but that her mind could not get any peace; and now she had come to ask Friends to release her for this service. One after another the

Friends would "concur in this concern," and the blessing of the Lord would be invoked upon the messenger who was going forth.

Some of these occasions were of a heavenly sort, and the voices of strong men choked in tears as a beloved brother or sister was equipped and set free. From this little meeting heralds went out to almost every part of the world, and the act of liberation was something never to be forgotten, and only to be surpassed by the deep rejoicing which stirred the same company when the journey was over and "the minutes were returned."

The turning point, though by no means the attainment, came for me in a very simple incident—of blessed memory. I had gone a step further than usual, and had done something which grieved everybody at home, and I expected a severe punishment, which was administered with extreme infrequency in our home. To my surprise my mother took me by the hand and led me to my room; then she solemnly kneeled down by me, and offered a prayer which reached the very inmost soul of me, and reached also the real Helper. No holy of holies would ever have seemed to the pious Jew more awful with the presence of God than that chamber seemed to me. It was one thing to hear prayer in the meetinghouse, or in the assembled family, but quite another thing to hear my own case laid before God in words which made me see just what I was, and no less clearly what I ought to be, and what with his help I might be. I learned that day what a mother was for! And though I was still far from won, I was at least where I could more distinctly feel the thread between my soul and the Father quiver and draw me.

I think that my Uncle Eli more than anybody else helped me to realize—not by what he said, but by what he did—that this goodness of character which I was after is not something miraculous that drops into a soul out of the skies, but is rather something which is formed within as one faithfully does his set tasks, and goes to work with an enthusiastic passion to help make other people good. I saw him growing white and bent with the advance of years, but no touch of age in the slightest degree weakened his efforts to make our neighborhood better. He preached the Gospel on the first day of the week, and the next day worked at a scheme for building up a town library. One day he was trying to do something to destroy the saloon and advance the cause of temperance, and the next he would be raising money to endow an educational institution. Now he would be busy organizing a local missionary society and the next day he might be advocating a better system of taxation for the town. If he drove by he might be on his way to the station to start off for an extended religious visit, or he might be going down the road to visit a sick neighbour. In all his work for the betterment of man at home and abroad, I never saw him discouraged or in doubt about the final issue. He was always full of hope and courage, and radiantly happy to be able to work at human problems.

But the thing which impressed me most, as a thoughtful boy, was that in all this perplexing and wearying work, he was becoming more and more like my ideal of a saint. His face was sunny; his smile was always ready to break out. We were all happier when he came, and he himself seemed to have a kind of inward peace which was very much like what I supposed the heavenly beings had. It had been his preaching which had so influenced my very early life; but it was much more his victorious life, which spoke with an unanswerable power like that of a sunset or the starry sky, that influenced me now in this critical time. I felt that the way to become good was to go to work in the power of God to help make others good, and to help solve the problems of those among whom we live.

I got a further impression of this truth from an event which came at first as a calamity. I went out one morning in early winter to feed our cattle and horses in the barn, and found to my horror that a fearful storm in the night had blown the barn down with almost everything we possessed in it. It was such a wreck as I had never seen. I can remember now the way I felt as I ran through the neighbourhood to call the men together to see if we could save anything. The news went fast, and before the day was over men from near and far gathered in our yard. They were all hardworking people like ourselves, with little wealth beyond their own strong hands. But before they separated they had decided to go to work at once and replace what the storm had destroyed. The entire neighbourhood went to work, and a new structure rose where the ruin had been.

It was a simple deed, which perhaps many towns could parallel, but it affected me in a strange way. I saw, as I had not seen before, that the religion of these men was not merely an affair of the meetinghouse; not merely a way to get to heaven. It was something which made them thoughtful of others and ready to sacrifice for others. I saw how it worked itself out in practical deeds of kindness and righteousness. During those days that I worked in the cold of a Maine winter, among those men with their rough clothes and hard hands, I was helping build more than a barn; I was forming a wider view of the religion which such men as these were living by.

The Luminous Trail

In the final chapter of Rufus Jones's book The Luminous Trail, which appeared the year before his death in 1948, he tells of the life and death of his son. He had been married in 1888 to his wife, Sarah Coutant. Their son was born in 1892, and his wife died of tuberculosis seven years later, leaving him to care for his little son.

— D.S.

The boy that I am writing about here . . . left me when he was only eleven years old. . . . The birth of this son in midwinter of 1892 was one of the supreme events of my life. He was named Lowell after my beloved poet. I took him in my arms from the doctor—which would not be allowed now in a modern hospital—and felt an unutterable emotion of joy and wonder. . . . I never got away from this divine miracle. There was light on this child's face which I did not put there. There were marks of heavenly origin too plain to miss. Poets admit that the child trails "clouds of glory from God who is our home," but they spoil it all by predicting that the glory will quickly "fade into the light of common day." It was not so with this child. A child looking at a beautiful object was told that it would soon be gone. "Never mind," he said, "there'll be something else beautiful tomorrow." The "light" kept growing plainer and more real through the eleven years he lived here on earth with me. It never became "common day."

The time came all too soon when I had to be both father and mother to this dear boy, and then the depth of fusion became even greater, and our lives grew together from within in a way that does not often happen. What I did for him cannot be known, but I live to say no human being could have done more to teach me the way of life than he did. He helped me to become simple and childlike, gentle and loving, confident and trustful.

All too soon this boy, "by the vision splendid on his way attended," came to an end here on earth where I could see him. He had diptheria in the spring of 1903. He was given anti-toxin and recovered, as far as we could see, completely. In July I went to England to lecture at the Quaker Summer School, which was to be the opening of the Woodbrooke Settlement at Selly Oak, near Birmingham. Lowell was to stay at his grandmother's home in Ardonia, New York, with a companion. He was always happy at Ardonia. . . . But the night before landing in Liverpool I awoke in my berth with a strange sense of trouble and sadness. As I lay wondering what it meant, I felt myself invaded by a Presence and held by the Everlasting Arms. It was the most extraordinary experience I had ever had. But I had no intimation that anything was happening to Lowell. When we landed in Liverpool a cable informed me that he was desperately ill, and a second cable in answer to one from me brought the dreadful news that he was gone.

When my sorrow was at its most acute stage I was walking along a great city highway [Birmingham], when suddenly I saw a little child come out of a great gate, which swung to and fastened behind her. She wanted to go to her home behind the gate, but it would not open. She pounded in vain with her little fist. She rattled the gate. Then she wailed as though her heart would break. The cry brought the mother. She caught the child in her arms and kissed away the tears. "Didn't you know I would come? It is all right now." All of a sudden I saw with my spirit that there was love behind my shut gate.

Yes, "where there is so much love, *there must be* more."

THE WRITINGS OF
THOMAS R. KELLY

Thomas R. Kelly (1893–1941)

Thomas R. Kelly has been spoken of as a Brother Lawrence of our time: one who brought the presence of God into the commonest acts of daily life. He grew up as a Quaker boy in Ohio. His Quaker mother, widowed when he was only four years old, had moved into the Quaker college town of Wilmington. There, by dint of her tireless labor and Tom's own vigilance at self-support, he ultimately studied and graduated. After graduate study at Haverford College and a Ph.D. in philosophy from Hartford Theological Seminary, he taught philosophy at Earlham College and, from 1936 until his early death in 1941, at Haverford College.

Following a crushing disappointment in the late autumn of 1937, Thomas Kelly was swept by an experience of the "Presence" where, in his own words, he tells us that he was "melted down by the Love of God." During the next three years, in a series of messages that were eventually printed in various Quaker publications, he poured out the prophetic insights that he had experienced and did so with an unmistakable authenticity. A few months after his death in January 1941, I edited and published a selection of these messages, calling the book A Testament of Devotion. Twenty-five years later, his son, Richard Kelly, published another small volume of additional papers with the apt title The Eternal Promise.

—DOUGLAS V. STEERE

The Eternal Promise

The straightest road to social gospel runs through profound mystical experience. The paradox of true mysticism is that individual experience leads to social passion, that the nonuseful engenders the greatest utility. If we seek a social gospel, we must find it most deeply rooted in the mystic way. Love of God and love of neighbor are not two commandments, but one. It is the highest experience of the mystic, when the soul of man is known to be one with God himself, that utility drops off and flutters away, useless, to earth, that world-shaking consciousness of mankind in need arises in one and he knows himself to be the channel of Divine Life. The birth of true mysticism brings with it the birthday of the widest social gospel. "American" Christianity is in need of this deeper strain of expression of direct contact with God, as the source, not of world-flight, but of the most intensely "practical" Christianity that has yet been known.

The Quaker discovery and message has always been that God still lives and moves, works and guides, in vivid immediacy, within the hearts of men. For revelation is not static and complete, like a book, but dynamic and enlarging, as springing from a Life and Soul of all things. This Light and Life is in all men, ready to sweep us into its floods, illumine us with its blinding, or with its gentle guiding radiance, send us tendered but strong into the world of need and pain and blindness. Surrender of self to that indwelling Life is entrance upon an astounding, an almost miraculous Life.

It is to have that mind in you which was also in Jesus Christ. "Behold, I stand at the door and knock." In the silence of your hearts hear him knock. Outward teachers can only lead us to the threshold. But "God himself has come to lead his people." Such men and women must be raised up, heaven-led souls who are not "seekers" alone, but "finders," finders who have been found by the Father of all the world's prodigals.

. . . How different is the experience of Life . . . when the Eternal Presence suffuses it! Suddenly, unexpectedly, we are lifted in a plateau of peace. The dinning clamor of daily events—so real, so urgent they have been!—is framed in a new frame, is seen from a new perspective. The former things are passed away; behold, they have become new. This world, our world, and its problems, does not disappear nor lose its value. It reappears in a new light, upheld in a new and amazingly quiet power. Calm replaces strain, peace replaces anxiety. Assurance, relaxation, and integration of life set in. With hushed breath we do our tasks. Reverently we live in the presence of the Holy. . . . Life itself becomes a sacrament wherein sin is blasphemy. A deep longing for personal righteousness and purity sets in. Old tempting weaknesses no longer appeal as they did before. In patience we smile in loving concern for those who rush about with excited desperation. Oh, why can they not see the ocean of light and love which flows completely over the ocean of darkness and death! But all things [are] in his Providence. A little taste of Cosmic Patience, which a Father-heart must have for a wayward world, becomes ours. The world's work is to be done. But it doesn't have to be finished by us.

We have taken ourselves too seriously. The life of God overarches *all* lifetimes.

🌾

The old self, the little self—how weak it is, and how absurdly confident and how absurdly timid it has been! How jealously we guard its strange precious pride! Famished for superiority-feeling, as Alfred Adler pointed out, its defeats must be offset by a dole of petty victories. In religious matters we still thought that we should struggle to present to God a suitable offering of service. We planned, we prayed, we suffered, we carried the burden. The we, the self, how subtly it intrudes itself into religion! And then steals in, so sweetly, so all replacing, the sense of Presence, the sense of Other, and he plans, and he bears the burdens, and we are a new creature. Prayer becomes not hysterical cries to a distant God, but gentle uplifting and faint whispers, in which it is not easy to say *who* is speaking, we, or an Other through us. Perhaps we can only say: praying is taking place. Power flows through us, from the Eternal into the rivulets of Time. Amazed, yet not amazed, we stride the stride of the tender giant who dwells within us, and wonders are performed. Active as never before, one lives in the passive voice, alert to be used, fearful of nothing, patient to stand and wait.

It is an amazing discovery, at first, to find that a creative Power and Life is at work in the world. God is no longer the object of a belief; he is a Reality, who has continued, within us, his real Presence in the world. God is aggressive. He is an intruder, a lofty lowly conqueror on whom we had counted too little, because we had counted on ourselves. Too long have we supposed that we must carry the banner of religion, that it was our concern. But religion is not our concern; it is God's concern. Our task is to call men to "be still, and know that I am God," to hearken to that of God within them, to invite, to unclasp the clenched fists of self-resolution, to be pliant in his firm guidance, sensitive to the inflections of the inner voice.

For there is a life beyond earnestness to be found. It is the life rooted and grounded in the Presence, the Life which has been found by the Almighty. Seek it, seek it. Yet it lies beyond seeking. It arises in being found. To have come only as far as religious determination is only to have stood in the vestibule. But our confidence in our shrewdness, in our education, in our talents, in some aspect or other of our self-assured self, is our own undoing. So earnestly busy with anxious, fevered efforts for the kingdom of God have we been, that we failed to hear the knock upon the door, and to know that our chief task is to open that door and be entered by the Divine Life.

There is an old, old story that the gateway to deep religion is self-surrender. Dr. Coomaraswamy, writing upon the art of India, says that all developed religions have as their center the experience of becoming unselfed. But falling in love is an old, old story in the history of the world, yet new to each individual when first it comes. Descriptions of the unselfing which comes with the Invading Love are no substitute for the immediacy of the experience of being unselfed by the Eternal Captain of our souls. Nor is there a freedom so joyous as the enslaving bonds of such amazing, persuading Love.

But according to our Christian conception of the unselfing in religion, to become unselfed is to become truly integrated as a richer self. The little, time-worn self about which we fretted—how narrow its boundaries, how unstable its base, how strained its structure. But the experience of discovering that life is rooted and grounded in the actual, active, loving Eternal One is also to experience our own personal life firm-textured and stable.

To you I speak with much hesitation about suffering. For I am only in middle years, and for me life has not been hard. But there is an introduction to suffering which comes with the birthpains of Love. And in such suffering one finds for the first time how deep and profound is the nature and meaning of life. And in such suffering one sees, as if one's eye were newly opened upon a blinding light, the very Life of the Eternal God himself. And there too is suffering, but there, above all, is peace and victory.

Another aspect of the same awakening of the soul-tenderness is the new love of the world. Before, we had loved the world because it enriched our lives—we were the receiving centers. But now all is new, even the nature of love itself. Our families, our dear ones, they are reloved.

Worship does not consist in achieving a mental state of concentrated isolation from one's fellows. But in the depth of common worship it is as if we found our separate lives were all one life, within whom we live and move and have our being. Communication seems to take place sometimes without words having been spoken. In the silence we received an unexpected commission to bear in loving intentness the spiritual need of another person sitting nearby. And that person goes away, uplifted and refreshed. Sometimes in that beautiful experience of living worship which the Friends have called "the gathered meeting," it is as if we joined hands and hearts, and lifted them together toward the unspeakable glory. Or it is as if that light and warmth dissolved us together into one. Tears are not to be scorned, then, for we stand together in the Holy of Holies.

A few weeks ago a man and his wife told me, with light in their eyes, how, three years ago, in the midst of their eighteen-year-old daughter's death had come to them the peace and Presence of the Great Companion, and had rebuilt them into lives of joyful service among young people of their daughter's generation. . . . From such people time's arrows fall back, like the spear of Klingsor hurled at the heart of Parsifal.

> For I am persuaded, that neither death, nor life, nor angels, nor principalities, nor powers, nor things present, nor things to come, nor height, nor depth, nor any other creature, shall be able to separate us from the love of God, which is in Christ Jesus our Lord. (Rom 8:38–39)

Secular action is on the increase and religion as an influence is on the wane. Quakers appeared in history at just such a time as this, when the experience of deep religion had grown thin. Preachers lacked personal relationship with God. The Society of Friends arose to bring back vital apostolic power. The purpose was not to form another sect and to justify it by a peculiar tenet. Friends came to dig down to the wellsprings of spiritual immediacy, holding that religion means that which you know, feel, experience within yourself. Our task isn't to nurse the dying embers of a dying sect, but to be missionaries to Christendom; to live in a real Christian fellowship, not within a definite organization.

We are men of double personalities. We have slumbering demons within us. We all have also a dimly-formed Christ within us. We've been too ready to say that the demonic man within us is the natural and the real man, and that the Christ-man within us is the unnatural and the unreal self. But the case is that our surface potentialities are for selfishness and greed, for tooth and claw. But deep within, in the whispers of the heart, is the surging call of the Eternal Christ, hidden within us all. By an inner isthmus we are connected with the mainland of the Eternal Love. Surface living has brought on the world's tragedy. Deeper living leads us to the Eternal Christ, hidden in us all. Absolute loyalty to this inner Christ is the only hope of a new humanity. In the clamor and din of the day, the press of Eternity's warm love still whispers in each of us, as our truest selves. Attend to the Eternal that he may re-create you and sow you deep into the furrows of the world's suffering.

Each one of us has the Seed of Christ within him. In each of us
the amazing and the dangerous Seed of Christ is present. It is
only a Seed. It is very small, like the grain of mustard seed. The
Christ that is formed in us is small indeed, but he is great with
eternity. But if we dare to take this awakened Seed of Christ into
the midst of the world's suffering, it will grow. That's why the
Quaker work camps are important. Take a young man or young
woman in whom Christ is only dimly formed, but one in whom
the Seed of Christ is alive. Put him into a distressed area, into a
refugee camp, into a poverty region. Let him go into the world's
suffering, bearing this Seed with him, and in suffering it will
grow, and Christ will be more and more fully formed in him. As
the grain of mustard seed grew so large that the birds found
shelter in it, so the man who bears an awakened Seed into the
world's suffering will grow until he becomes a refuge for many.

The early Quakers were founding no sect; they were reforming
Christendom, that had slumped into externals and had lost its
true sense of the immediate presence and the creative, triumphant power of the living God within us all. They had a message for all, for they had discovered that "the Lord himself had
come to lead his people."

And in that same way the Quaker discovery, not of a doctrine,
not of a belief, but of a Life, a life filled with God, a life listening,
obedient, triumphant, holy—in that same way the Quaker discovery was only a rediscovery of the life and power and fellow-

ship and joy and radiance which moved the early Church. Its rediscovery today is desperately needed, for the fellowship of believers has grown dim, and only a few clear voices ring out in the twilight. You and I can be the instruments of the opening of God's life. But it is heroic work, not work for the milder Quaker. The fires of God burn bright. In their light we are judged or consumed, in their light the world is condemned. In their light we may discover what so many have really lost, namely, God himself. And what is a greater discovery?

In the practice of group worship on the basis of silence come special times when the electric hush and solemnity and depth of power steals over the worshipers. A blanket of divine covering comes over the room, a stillness that can be felt is over all, and the worshipers are gathered into a unity and synthesis of life which is amazing indeed. A quickening Presence pervades us, breaking down some part of the special privacy and isolation of our individual lives and blending our spirits within a superindividual Life and Power. An objective, dynamic Presence enfolds us all, nourishes our souls, speaks glad, unutterable comfort within us, and quickens us in depths that had before been slumbering. The Burning Bush has been kindled in our midst, and we stand together on holy ground.

Such gathered meetings I take to be cases of group mysticism. . . . The gathered meeting I take to be of the same kind, still milder and more diffused, yet really of a piece with all mystical experience. For mystical times are capable of all gradings and shadings, from sublime heights to very mild moments of lift and very faint glimpses of glory. In the gathered meeting the sense is present that a new life and Power has entered our midst. And we know not only that we stand erect in the holy Presence, but also that others sitting with us are experiencing the same exaltation and access of power. We may not know these our neighbors in any outwardly intimate sense, but we now know them, as it were, from within, and they know us in the same way, as souls now alive in the same areas and as blended into the body of Christ, which is his church. Again and again this community of life and guidance from the Presence in the midst is made clear by the way the spoken words uttered in the meeting join on to one another and to our inward thoughts. This, I presume, has been a frequent experience for us all, as a common life and current sweeps through all. We are in communication with one another because we are being communicated to, and through, by the Divine Presence.

I believe that the group mysticism of the gathered meeting rests upon the Real Presence of God in our midst. Quakers generally hold to a belief in Real Presence, as firm and solid as the belief of Roman Catholics in the Real Presence in the host, the bread and the wine of the Mass. In the host the Roman Catholic is convinced that the literal, substantial Body of Christ is present. For him the Mass is not a mere symbol, a dramatizing of some figurative relationship of man to God. It rests upon the persuasion that an Existence, a Life, the Body of Christ, is really present and entering into the body of man. Here the Quaker is very near the

Roman Catholic. For the Real Presence of the gathered meeting is an existential fact. To use philosophical language, it is an ontological matter, not merely a psychological matter. The bond of union in divine fellowship is existential and real, not figurative. It is the life of God himself, within whose life we live and move and have our being. And the gathered meeting is a special case of holy fellowship of the blessed community.

One condition for such a group experience seems to be this: some individuals need already, upon entering the meeting, to be gathered deep in the spirit of worship. There must be some kindled hearts when the meeting begins. In them, and from them, begins the work of worship. The spiritual devotion of a few persons, silently deep in active adoration, is needed to kindle the rest, to help those others who enter the service with tangled, harried, distraught thoughts to be melted and quieted and released and made pliant, ready for the work of God and his Real Presence.

In power and labor one lifts the group, in inward prayer, high before the throne. With work of soul the kindled praying worshiper holds the group, his comrades and himself, high above the sordid and trivial, and prays in quiet, offering that Light may drive away the shadows of self-will. Where this inward work of upholding prayer is wholly absent, I am not sure that a gathered meeting is at all likely to follow.

He who carries a Shekinah [presence of God] daily in his heart, and practices continual retirement within that Shekinah, *at the*

same time as he is carrying on his daily affairs, has begun to prepare for worship, for he has never ceased worshiping. Such worship is no intermittent process, but a foundation layer of the life of the children of the kingdom. And such a special sense of bondedness and unity with others as is experienced in the gathered meeting is only a time of particular enhancement of the life of bondedness and fellowship in love among souls which is experienced daily, as we carry one another in inward upholding prayer.

A second condition concerns the spoken words of the meeting. Certainly the deepness of the covering of a meeting is not proportional to the number of words spoken. A gathered meeting may proceed entirely in silence, rolling on with increasing depth and intensity until the meeting breaks and tears are furtively brushed away. Such really powerful hours of unbroken silence frequently carry a genuine progression of spiritual change and experience.

But I have more particularly in mind those hours of worship in which no one person, no one speech, stands out as the one that "made" the meeting, those hours wherein the personalities that take part verbally are not enhanced as individuals in the eyes of others, but are subdued and softened and lost sight of because in the language of Fox, "the Lord's power was over all." Brevity, earnestness, sincerity—and frequently a lack of polish—characterized the best Quaker speaking. The words should rise like a shaggy crag upthrust from the surface of silence, under the pressure of river power and yearning, contrition, and wonder. But on the other hand the words should not rise up like a shaggy crag. They should not break the silence, but continue it. For the Divine Life who is ministering through the medium of silence is the same Life as is now ministering through words. And when such words are truly spoken "in the Life," then when such words cease, the uninterrupted silence and worship continue, for silence and words have been of one texture, one piece. Second and third speakers only continue the enhancement of the moving Presence, until a climax is reached, and the discerning head of the meeting knows when to break it.

But what if the meeting has not been a gathered meeting? Are those meetings failures that have not been hushed by a covering? Quite definitely they are not. If *we have been* faithful, we may go home content and nourished from any meeting.

Like the individual soul, the group must learn to endure spiritual weather without dismay. Some hours of worship are full of glow and life, but others lack the quality. The disciplined soul, and the disciplined group, have learned to cling to the reality of God's Presence, whether the feeling of Presence is great or faint. If only the group has been knit about the very springs of motivation, the fountain of the will, then real worship has taken place.

To you in this room who are seekers, to you, young and old who have toiled all night and caught nothing, but who want to launch out into deeps and let down your nets for a draught, I want to speak, as simply, as tenderly, as clearly as I can. For God can be found. There is a last Rock for your souls, a resting place of absolute peace and joy and power and radiance and security. There is a Divine Center into which your life can slip, a new and absolute orientation to God, a Center where you live with him, and out from which you see all of life, through new and radiant vision, tinged with new sorrows and pangs, new joys unspeakable and full of glory.

ABOUT THE EDITOR

HarperCollins Spiritual Classics Series Editor Emilie Griffin has long been interested in the classics of the devotional life. She has written a number of books on spiritual formation and transformation, including *Clinging: The Experience of Prayer* and *Wilderness Time: A Guide to Spiritual Retreat*. With Richard J. Foster she coedited *Spiritual Classics: Selected Readings on the Twelve Spiritual Disciplines*. Her latest book is *Wonderful and Dark Is this Road: Discovering the Mystic Path*. She is a board member of Renovaré and leads retreats and workshops throughout the United States. She and her husband, William, live in Alexandria, Louisiana.

ABOUT RICK MOODY

Rick Moody, author of the Foreword, is the author of the novels *Garden State*, *The Ice Storm*, and *Purple America*; two collections of stories, *The Ring of Brightest Angels Around Heaven* and *Demonology*; and a nonfiction work, *The Black Veil*. His new novel, *The Diviners*, will be published in early 2006.

THE CLASSICS OF **WESTERN SPIRITUALITY**
A LIBRARY OF THE GREAT SPIRITUAL MASTERS

These volumes contain original writings of universally acknowledged teachers within the Catholic, Protestant, Eastern Orthodox, Jewish, Islamic, and American Indian traditions.

The Classics of Western Spirituality unquestionably provide the most in-depth, comprehensive, and accessible panorama of Western mysticism ever attempted. From the outset, the Classics has insisted on the highest standards for these volumes, including new translations from the original languages, and helpful introductions and other aids by internationally recognized scholars and religious thinkers, designed to help the modern reader to come to a better appreciation of these works that have nourished the three monotheistic faiths for centuries.

  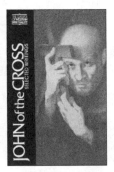 

For more information on the
CLASSICS OF WESTERN SPIRITUALITY, **contact Paulist Press**
(800) 218-1903 • www.paulistpress.com